50 WAYS TO HELP YOUR CHURCH GROW

'Christ loved the church and gave himself up for her.'
(Ephesians 5:25)

D1350289

Commendations

David Beer is a winner when it comes to church growth in the British context. Every church he has served, from Coventry to Gravesend, to Tonbridge, to Frinton-on-Sea, has experienced substantial growth under his leadership. And, each time, this growth occurred in a context of overall decline in mainline denominational churches.

I had the privilege of serving with David Beer as his associate for three years in Tonbridge. Much that I learned about leadership and team ministry was under his tutelage. I am forever indebted to my friend and mentor, who continues to pattern successful ministry in a style which is winsome and is biblically based in orientation.

You do well to read with a disciple's heart the seasoned counsel contained within these pages. If Britain is to experience a new day in church growth and advance in Kingdom causes, it will occur in part because the churches embody the purpose-driven principles identified in this book. They work because they are spiritually sound and culturally relevant.

Dr Larry Michael,
Senior Minister, First Baptist Church,
Clanton, Alabama.

My friend David Beer has written a wonderfully practical and inspiring application of the purpose-driven paradigm for UK churches. This is a book filled with hope! If put into practice, I believe it could bring about a mighty spiritual awakening that could touch every city and town and bring many to Christ. May God give it a wide readership!

Rick Warren, pastor and author of *The Purpose-Driven Church.*

Pastor David Beer has struck a resounding chord in his new book. He has harmoniously blended spiritual principles of church life with practical programs that make for solid growth and Kingdom extension. Pastors, church leaders or lay persons will find it challenging, inspiring and truly helpful. I must enthusiastically recommend it to all readers.

Dr Lewis A. Drummond,
Billy Graham Chair of Evangelism,
Beeson Divinity School, Samford University.

50 Ways to Help Your Church Grow

DAVID BEER

EASTBOURNE

First published 2000
Reprinted 2000, 2001

ISBN 0 85476 810 6

Published by
KINGSWAY PUBLICATIONS
Lottbridge Drove, Eastbourne, BN23 6NT, England.
Email: books@kingsway.co.uk

Designed and produced for the publishers by
Bookprint Creative Services, P.O. Box 827, BN21 3YJ, England.
Printed in Great Britain.

Contents

To my granddaughter, Brianna.
May she fulfil the potential
God has placed in her life.

Acknowledgements

In 1997 I took a sabbatical. I am grateful to both the Baptist Union and Frinton Free Church for allowing me this period of study and travel.

The 25,000 word paper which resulted from my sabbatical has been the basis of this book. I would like to thank those who have encouraged and supported me in getting the task completed, and especially Dorothy, my wife and partner in ministry for over thirty years. I would also like to thank our children Leisa and Keith who have never stopped encouraging and praying for me, and my enthusiastic son-in-law, the Revd Steve Rouse, Minister of Balham Baptist Church.

Dr Lewis Drummond, my mentor and friend, with whom I served in the ministry of the great 'Ninth-and-0' Baptist Church in Louisville, Kentucky, has been a big influence on my life. So also have the churches I have served in the UK: Meredith Road Baptist Church, Coventry; Emmanuel Baptist Church, Gravesend; Tonbridge Baptist Church; and Frinton Free Church. I am blessed to be Senior Pastor of Frinton Free Church, a Baptist church that has caught the vision of many of the principles described in this book.

I have learned much from church leaders with whom I have served and from those who have been my associates, especially

Larry Michael and Steve Chalke, both of whom served with me in Tonbridge, and Derek Moon and David Hibbin who served with me at Frinton. I am also grateful to members of the wider team of leaders who have served these churches as elders and deacons, for their forgiveness of my failures, their patience with my mistakes, and their encouragement of my strengths.

Finally, I would like to say thank you to Pastor Rick Warren, for his inspiration and encouragement. Rick loves pastors and has committed his life to assisting and encouraging them, especially those who serve in small churches. I recommend that you visit the two web sites of Saddleback Valley Community Church, California: www.pastors.com and www.saddleback.com

Foreword

'Never buy a cure for baldness from a man wearing a wig.' Good advice not just for those struggling with what we politely refer to as 'hair loss' but far more widely as an important life principle.

Put another way, be very careful who you listen to. The ability to deliver persuasive arguments is far more common than that of being able to deliver the goods. Put cynically, we are all desperately afraid that the old adage is still true – 'those who can, do; those who can't, teach'…

I first worked with David when I was 20, have known him for almost a quarter of a century, and have seen him consistently 'deliver the goods'. I joined him in his second pastorate at Gravesend Baptist Church in the mid 1970s and worked there for a year before entering theological college to begin my own formal training for the Baptist ministry. After four years at Spurgeon's College I then worked with David as an associate pastor for four years at Tonbridge Baptist Church.

After we had both left Tonbridge we worked together again in another capacity. David, as well as serving as Senior Minister at Frinton Free Church in Essex, has been a religious adviser for Anglia Television and worked on the production team for ITV's *Sunday Morning* programme. David introduced me to the

opportunity to take part in a Sunday morning television programme produced by Anglia TV for the ITV network. That led
to further opportunities with both ITV and the BBC.

On January 2nd, 2000, we had another opportunity to work
together, this time through Fanfare for a New Generation, on
the first ITV televised worship service of the new millennium.
Fanfare is a Christian charity encouraging local Christians to
engage their faith with local communities. David's church,
Frinton Free Church, is one of a number of churches across the
country that has risen to Fanfare's New Millennium Challenge
– ten goals that encourage local churches to be more welcoming, relevant and challenging.

David's conviction is that God wants every church to grow,
both spiritually and numerically. David has served in churches
of varying sizes, which have always grown. His vision has been
of a church that reaches out to the community and the world.

In this book David talks about the key principles he has followed over the years that have led to the growth of his present
church. Frinton Free Church is built on a foundation of prayer.
It is a church that, without compromising the Christian
message, is relevant and welcoming to the community, and
through television, radio and print has made a witness to the
nation as a whole.

The book highlights some of the typical patterns and causes
of decline in attendance that characterized British churches in
the twentieth century, and invites a fresh way of looking at the
local church with its enormous potential to radically influence
the values of our culture.

Many books spell out the principles of building healthy
churches, but few actually tell you how to apply those principles. This is not a book about new ways of doing things.
Neither does it offer a quick-fix to the problems that plague
declining churches. It gathers together tried and tested biblically based practical principles, the sum of which provides us
with the tools to get many churches out of the rut of spiritual

dryness and irrelevance and on the road to health and growth.

The local church has enormous potential and one that must be unleashed if the Christian community is to fulfil its purpose in the community and the world. This book provides a starting point for any church leader who desires to fulfil Christ's Great Commission to make disciples and incorporate them into the family of God and in turn influence the society and culture in which we live at the beginning of the twenty-first century.

Revd Steve Chalke
Founding Director, Oasis Trust

1

Unleashing the Potential of Your Church

With the long, wide tarmac runway stretching ahead the four-seater aircraft was ready for take-off. The four people on board were excited about their flight across the English Channel for a day trip to France. As the aircraft waited for clearance, the pilot's hand on the power lever, ready to push forward to full power, the air traffic controller uttered those decisive words, 'Cleared for take-off'.

I was the pilot. Having qualified a few years earlier, I had never quite got over the anticipation of waiting to hear those liberating words. The exhilaration of unleashing the aircraft for flight. The sound of the engine springing into life at full power. The thrust forward as the aircraft quickly accelerated down the broad runway. The feel of the aircraft as it reached for the air and climbed into the sky. Suddenly everything around seemed different. The aircraft was doing what it was designed to do. This was its natural environment. It had moved slowly and awkwardly on the ground; now it was fulfilling its potential.

In the same way, there is a strong desire for local churches to unleash their potential and fulfil the purpose for which they were designed. The purpose of every aircraft is to fly; that's what it's designed to do. But each type of aircraft has its own specific purposes too. In the same way, the overall purpose of the church is clearly defined in the Bible, but each local church needs to define its own purposes to reach that goal.

Every pilot knows that two thirds of an aircraft's lift into the air comes from the air above the wings and only one third of its lift comes from the air below the wings. As the air flows over the upper curved surface of the wings, so the air pressure above the wings is reduced and the aircraft is literally sucked upwards. Our lift comes from above. Our purpose is defined in heaven. Our power comes from God, but like the pilot of an aircraft, there is a need to know just how to apply it.

A pilot needs aeronautical knowledge. He or she needs to know about the four forces that act on a plane while it is in straight and level flight: *lift*, the upward thrusting force; *weight* or *gravity*, the downward acting force; *thrust*, the forward acting force; and *drag*, the backward acting, or retarding force of wind resistance.

To understand how lift is produced, the pilot must understand a phenomenon discovered years ago by the scientist Bernoulli and later called Bernoulli's Principle: the pressure of a fluid (liquid or gas) decreases at points where the speed of the fluid increases. In other words, Bernoulli found that within the same fluid, in this case air, high speed of flow is associated with low pressure, and low speed with high pressure.

A pilot needs this knowledge. However, when I was learning to fly 3,000 feet up in the sky and my flight instructor said, 'You have control,' it was not Bernoulli's Principle that was on my mind. It was my sweaty palms as I took over the controls of the aircraft. I was more concerned about placing my feet on the correct point on the rudder pedals, how much pressure I needed to use on the aileron and elevator control, whether or not I was gaining or losing height, and if I was travelling in the right direction.

In a similar way, a minister or pastor needs as good a biblical and theological education as possible, but when it comes to ministry and the actual leading of a church, a whole new dimension faces us – just how do we go about building a strong, healthy church?

This book is not written by a theologian, a college lecturer, a church-growth specialist or, dare I say, a North American pastor of a mega-church. It is written by an ordinary UK pastor who has worked with the everyday demands of ministry in six different churches in six different social and cultural contexts.

As a local pastor I see myself as a general practitioner. I know that others, like myself, want to know how to bridge the gap between ministerial formation, theological education, strategies for evangelism and mission that sometimes seem so complex, and actually getting the job done. We want a starting point.

As a place to begin, I offer four principles which are the four parts of this book. They are not new, but in some churches they may have been forgotten and need to be revisited. In other places they may need to be more clearly identified and shaped to fit the purposes of the church. They have not solved all the problems of church life, but they have contributed towards building healthy churches in each of my pastorates. Each principle fans out to take in other principles, as many or as few as you decide are appropriate and relevant.

I have learned much from other pastors and church leaders. I have drawn on the experience of many authors of books on church health. I have had the opportunity to visit hundreds of churches throughout my ministry. I am left with one strong conviction. In most instances, the potential of the local church, whatever its size, is enormous and unfulfilled. It has God's power to influence the community, and, in partnership with other local churches, the entire nation and the world.

Church leaders and their congregations are aware of the potential of the church. This book is not about that. Many fine definitions have been given already. For example:

In a world where there is disunity and fragmentation of every kind, the church offers genuine community. In a world where there is alienation and war the church witnesses to reconciliation and peace. In a world where there is hatred and evil the church's lifeblood is love and harmony. As a result of the finished work of Christ on the cross believers are to realise they are God's new society. He wants the church to be a visual aid before a watching world.[1]

Nothing impacts society so profoundly as a sustained period of true spiritual revival. The leadership of the church plays a vital role in such movements of the Holy Spirit. True spiritual revival comes only from God, but the church has a key part to play in recognizing and encouraging the principles God uses to stimulate and sustain spiritual and numerical growth. The church 'was strengthened; and encouraged by the Holy Spirit, it grew in numbers, living in the fear of the Lord' (Acts 9:31).

To unleash this powerful potential of the local church, we must translate fine ideals into everyday practical reality. This is something that many of us struggle with. Someone wrote to me about their own church situation:

It's difficult to be specific about future direction. Continuing to develop in prayer and growing in unity facilitate so much, and no doubt God will use these opportunities to continue to lead us. I long to see more of God at work.

So often we aspire to biblical ideals, but lack the application in a specific and purposeful way of the principles and power that God has provided. As someone said when they heard good points made in a sermon, 'Yes but how?'

Unleashing the potential of the church implies that its gifts and power lie dormant. Paul urged Timothy: 'Do not neglect your gift' (1 Timothy 4:14), and 'fan into flame the gift of God' (2 Timothy 1:6). Peter writes: 'Each one should use whatever

[1] David Coffey, *Build That Bridge*, Kingsway 1986, p. 50.

gift he has received to serve others, faithfully administering God's grace in its various forms. . . . If anyone serves, he should do it with the strength God provides . . .' (1 Peter 4:10–11). After Paul has urged the Christians in Rome to use their gifts to the full, he says: 'Never be lacking in zeal, but keep your spiritual fervour, serving the Lord' (Romans 12:11).

Every week about 1,500 people leave British churches. That doesn't include those who die or are transferred to other churches.[2] In 1980 the combined membership of all churches in the UK was 7.5 million. In 1990, it was 6.3 million. If the trend continues, it will soon be under 6 million. Even though many churches have experienced 'renewal', and even though there are large national celebrations for Christians of all traditions, for the most part the church in the UK is declining.

There is a mountain of books on the mission of the church. There are books that diagnose the spiritual state of our nation. There are books on leadership styles, how to initiate and manage change, and on issues of church health generally. Many of these books are excellent but sometimes, having read them in theological college, pastors now facing the demands of actual ministry are looking for practical, everyday principles to implement. I do not believe they are looking for a quick fix, but in my experience of talking with pastors, particularly those in the early years of ministry, their question is: 'Where do I begin?' Many church leaders genuinely want their church to grow into a healthy, fully functioning biblical community, but they need a starting point. And that is the purpose of this book.

---

[2] Philip Richter and Leslie Francis, *Gone But Not Forgotten*, Darton, Longman & Todd 1998.

2

Applying the Power

When I was learning to fly and the aircraft was cleared for take-off, the instructor sitting next to me would say authoritatively, 'Full power.' That meant a number of things: I had to push the throttle forward to its fullest extent with my right hand, keep my left hand on the controls ready to ease the aircraft into the air, while keeping both feet on the rudder pedals to maintain a straight course down the runway. The power needed to be connected to the principles of flight. Jesus had told the disciples: 'But you will receive power when the Holy Spirit comes on you; and you will be my witnesses in Jerusalem, and in all Judea and Samaria, and to the ends of the earth' (Acts 1:8). That power works when connected to the biblical principles that build a healthy church. The power needs to be wedded to the word. Jesus said to the Sadducees: 'Are you not in error because you do not know the Scriptures or the power of God?' (Mark 12:24). We need both.

In one church the members had met together to consider their future. Every Sunday saw decreasing attendance. They had no children, no youth; the congregation seemed predominantly elderly. A number of options were shared: 'Let's canvass the area with invitations to church'; 'Let's have a week of mission with a well-known evangelist'; 'What we need is revival'; 'An outpouring of the Holy Spirit would do it'. The last two suggestions certainly found an echo among those present. It seemed the problem was solved. A fresh outpouring of the Spirit was what was really needed. They could all go home.

What was missing was the application of power. The Holy Spirit was given in order that the disciples might be witnesses. The disciples were to join with Christ, through the Holy Spirit, to continue the work he had begun. It would be his power, but he was going to use them in this great journey of building his church.

Further into the New Testament, the apostle Paul shows clearly how to apply the power: accept what is our part and what is God's part, 'I planted the seed, Apollos watered it, but God made it grow' (1 Corinthians 3:6). Only God can make the church grow. But we need to apply the principles of growth.

The same practical principle is applied in the parable of the growing seed. Jesus said:

This is what the kingdom of God is like. A man scatters seed on the ground. Night and day, whether he sleeps or gets up, the seed sprouts and grows, though he does not know how. All by itself the soil produces corn – first the stalk, and then the ear, then the full kernel in the ear. As soon as the grain is ripe, he puts the sickle to it, because the harvest has come. (Mark 4:26–9)

Notice the connection. As Christian Schwarz (a Lutheran and head of the Institute for Church Development in Germany) points out in his book *Natural Church Development*:

This parable clearly shows what people can and should do, and what they cannot do. They should sow and harvest. What they cannot do is this: they cannot bring forth the fruit. I understand this principle to be the very essence of church growth. Some do it deliberately, others by instinct. It doesn't really matter. Ultimately, what counts is applying this principle.[1]

Schwarz asks: 'How should we view the opinion of Christians who profess that "all we can do for church development is to pray"?' He comments that this phrase is

> both theologically and empirically untenable. Many Bible passages illustrate that we can do much more for church development than just pray. We should, however, try to understand what people holding those convictions really want to say. They do not mean that we can do absolutely nothing but pray. They mean, 'Unless prayer, devotion to Christ, and a personal relationship with him are at the centre of all our activities, our striving amounts only to unfruitful "busyness".' And that is absolutely right.[2]

Theological insight has practical consequences. Thom Rainer has said:

> Christians who are filled with the Spirit are obedient Christians. All of the imperatives of Scripture become a joyful opportunity. Disciple-making (Matthew 28:19) becomes a way of life as many are won to Christ and the church grows daily.[3]

The principles mentioned in this book are not an attempt to build the church in our own strength. On the contrary. Implementing the biblical and spiritual principles of being a healthy, growing church is like setting the sails so that 'God might send us the powerful wind of his Holy Spirit. Then we might . . . discover that God likes nothing better than to answer those prayers.'[4] A later chapter emphasizes the powerful potential of prayer and how to develop a prayer ministry in the church.

---

[1] Christian Schwarz, *Natural Church Development*, Church Smart Resources 1996, p. 12.
[2] *Ibid.*, p. 106.
[3] Thom S. Rainer, *The Book of Church Growth*, Broadman 1993, p. 119.
[4] Schwarz, *Natural Church Development*, pp. 126–7.

An urgent need

There is no need to recount further the jarring statistics of declining church attendance in the UK. For most of the twentieth century, church attendance in Britain has been in steady decline. By contrast, in the second half of the twentieth century there was rapid growth in South America, Africa, Korea and China.

> Never before in human history has a voluntary movement grown as rapidly as Christianity is growing today. Without the aid of political or military forces the message of the kingdom of God is breaking frontiers in vast areas of Asia, Africa and Latin America with extraordinary church growth following. . . . Among Pentecostals, the most rapid growth has taken place in Latin America.[5]

It has been a different story in the UK and it is not the purpose of this book to identify or analyse the causes; many writers have done so already. But the urbanization of Britain and two world wars have undoubtedly contributed to this decline.

The story of an evangelical church in the north of England is typical of many. The church grew considerably in the second half of the nineteenth century. Its history records that

> this was a period when religious observance was both popular and respectable. Rev. Lauderdale preached with spiritual fervour and evangelical zeal which resulted in a continuous stream of applications for baptism and church membership, so that the chapel and schoolroom were soon bursting at the seams.

This growth led, in 1877, to a new building seating 1,150. On the day it was opened, it was not only filled but overflowed. 'Such was the spirit and fervour of that day over 400 people

---

[5] Rainer, *The Book of Church Growth*, p. 302.

attended a prayer meeting at 7 a.m. to ask God's blessing on the services which were to follow.' In January 1879 an evangelistic mission saw

> 1700 crowded into the building and many more were obliged to go away. . . . Sundays were busy days. The services would include a Prayer Meeting at 7.30 am, Morning Sunday School at 9.30 am, Morning Preaching Service 10.30 am, Afternoon Sunday School, Young Men's Bible Class and Young Women's Bible Class all at 2.00 pm, Open Air Meeting 5.30 pm, Evening Preaching Service at 6.00 pm, and Evening Prayer and Praise at 7.30 pm.

The history of this church goes on to state:

> There are indications that church attendance was showing signs of declining in the first decade of the new century and this trend was certainly not helped by the disruption of the War in the second decade. Sunday School attendances had fallen drastically in 1920 compared with forty years before.

From 1925 until 1934 'concern over decreasing congregations and a financial deficit steadily grew. It is true that there were occasions when the glories of bygone days were revived but only too fleetingly.' After the Second World War, 'the magnificent buildings erected in the previous century were now a burden on the diminished membership as renovations and redecoration became necessary'. Eventually, in 1955 the church agreed to sell the premises and find a new site. The new building was much smaller.

> In March 1960, it was decided to hold Sunday School experimentally on Sunday mornings and link it to morning worship in an attempt to establish Family Church. This proved successful and was therefore continued on a permanent basis.

The story is familiar to many churches in the UK during the twentieth century. Secularization shaped the cultural climate of the UK, drawing its strength from the spread of relative affluence, heightened material comfort and security, improvements in medicine and lengthened life expectancy. These factors reduced people's awareness of dependence on God, making religious belief not so much untrue as apparently unnecessary.

Sadly, in this environment, many British churches failed to communicate the relevance of the gospel effectively. Postmodernism, with its emphasis on the search for faith and spirituality, particularly since the sudden and dramatic death of Princess Diana, in some ways has not made the task any easier. Part of that search includes a rejection of the church.

Each chapter in the book *The Search for Faith and the Witness of the Church* starts with a statement by someone who is not a churchgoer. This one speaks for many:

My name's Adam. I think it's up to me to decide what's right – work it out for myself. I know there's God, but it's God getting through to me, not driving me to join up to some organisation. I believe in lots of things, karma and reincarnation and that. It makes sense when you look at it, right?

I'm really worried about what we're doing to the world and how we're destroying it. I think the earth talks to us and that the earth is full of power. I've done cards, pyramids, stones – and all that turns out pretty hopeful for me. I like to glimpse the future. I feel like I'm in control of my destiny. I like to work out, too, to feel good, really alive, right? Then I'll have a good massage to chill out, let myself go. Or meditate, be quiet. Then I know it's God telling me it's OK, it really is.

I don't need Church. You have to believe the party line, but I've worked all this out for myself. I want to pray and worship what I want in my own way and the Church doesn't give me that.[6]

---

[6] *The Search for Faith and the Witness of the Church*, Church House Publishing 1996.

The BBC's annual *Week of Faith* programmes offer a choice of faiths to the listeners. The mood among many is that as long as you find something to believe in, it doesn't matter what it is. It's up to you. Tolerance of each other's beliefs is of paramount importance.

To a large extent, the church has failed to understand the development of this mindset, and has even shown a reluctance to do so. Most Christian communicators find such thinking foreign and unfamiliar. Generally speaking, the church in the UK has failed to sustain the relevance of the gospel in a rapidly changing society.

> Given the pace of renewal over the last twenty years, the revitalisation of many churches, the growth in the large celebration gatherings and festivals, the resurgence of a voice in the corridors of power, you could be forgiven for viewing the state of the Church as essentially healthy and growing. However, this is not the case, the Church in the most part is declining and at best holding its own. Where there is growth, most of it seems to be a game of 'pass the saints'; when the music stops that's the church you end up in.[7]

The story of Frinton Free Church

This is where I serve as senior pastor at the time of writing. The church began in 1891, a late starter compared to many churches. Perhaps that gave it some advantages. Very quickly it needed a larger building than the small lecture hall in which the church worshipped in its first years. 'So began the endeavour to give effect to the vision of a permanent and commodious building worthy of the Church and town.'[8]

The building was formally opened on Tuesday 29th May 1912 at the heart of Frinton-on-Sea in Essex. However, in con-

---

[7] Revd Roger Sutton, *The Mission Files*, published occasionally by the Baptist Union of Great Britain.
[8] Derrick Whybrew, *The Story of Frinton Free Church*, Frinton, 1990.

trast to the previous building which had been far too small and overcrowded, the new building was never filled. Throughout Britain, the First World War shattered dreams. People were moved away from Frinton, visitors no longer came, and the church hall was taken over by soldiers. 'The church found itself without a minister and its membership scattered far and wide and one of its buildings under the control of the military – all that within four years of the opening ceremony.' Only a few members were left.

Between 1921 and 1926, in common with other churches in the country, attendance began to grow again. However, in Frinton, this was partly due to a minister who was described as 'a preacher of outstanding pulpit power'. During his ministry, the baptistry was used for the very first time since it was built! The growth of the church continued through the 1930s, under the leadership of another 'outstanding evangelical preacher'. However, in March 1935, the membership stood at only about 130. Then came the Second World War, and in 1940 the congregation was suddenly reduced to 20!

After the war the church grew back to a membership of 90, which continued to grow until it was approximately 120 in 1955. In 1965 it was about 220, and in 1975 it was 280. At the end of 1986 it was approximately 380. The church was going against the national trend. The years since 1945 were years of growth, both numerically and spiritually. In the 1970s and 80s, strong leadership produced a regular teaching ministry, both on Sundays and during the week, that resulted in a full church most weekends.

The church then found itself at a level of numerical growth where it would either stay the same for a number of years and then decline, or it would grow. It is common for British churches to stick at around 300 to 500 members for many years, until they start to decline. Continuing to grow and break the barrier of 500 to 600 would not be easy. There is a growth barrier every 50 to 100 members, and each one has to be negotiated carefully, but those above 500 seem particularly difficult to go through, perhaps because it's a long time since larger churches were common in the UK.

It wasn't easy to research the numerical growth of the church. As with other churches I researched, looking through old magazines and record books I discovered plenty of information about money, but congregation and membership statistics seemed never to be mentioned. It was easy to get the impression that money was counted, but people weren't.

As I built on the strong foundations of the ministry of my predecessor, the Revd Donald Bridge (under whose leadership the church had already rapidly grown), over 400 people joined the church during a period of ten years. For churches that have reached anywhere between 300 and 600 members, the question is what happens next. A number of issues were raised such as the overall health of the church, its organizational structure, the role of leaders, effective pastoral care, worship, and the general direction and purpose of the church.

To enable the growth to continue, the church agreed to upgrade the buildings. A balcony and a redesigned entrance were built to accommodate extra people. However, the outreach of the church during the week meant that it embarked on a much needed rebuilding project. By 1989 the buildings had been extensively altered, some parts being completely rebuilt. It was a step of faith that God honoured, enabling the church to be much more a part of the community in the town centre where it is located.

Buildings are only tools, but if you have them, they need to be relevant to the church's mission to the community. Of far greater importance was that members were willing to staff a weekday reception area with an open-door policy. The church office was staffed and became a point of communication. Until 1986 there wasn't even a telephone, let alone an office. In three of my previous churches, the first thing I did was ask for a telephone and a room to work in, as these basic requirements were absent. Now the tools for the ministry of the church include a staffed office, the usual computers, telephones, fax machine, and photocopier. Gradually we increased the full-time paid pastoral staff and the volunteer staff. A youth pastor and an associate pastor were added.

In the early 1990s there was still a problem of overcrowding. We started a second Sunday morning congregation for a trial period of eight weeks during the summer. The service was at 9 a.m. and we decided to keep it the same as the 11 a.m. service – the same sermon, hymns and songs. We believed this was an important principle, providing the two congregations with a sense of unity. When members of the two congregations met one another during the week, they knew they had worshipped in similar ways and shared the same sermon. I have seen too many churches divide themselves with two different styles of worship, creating the wrong kind of competition, often leading to conflict that was not handled constructively.

Starting another worship service can be difficult. How many people would attend the early service? On the first Sunday between 60 and 70 people were there. At the end of eight weeks, we sensed a reluctance to squeeze back into one service, but we did. The following year we ran the early second service for a longer period, stopping it just before winter. By this time, we had a congregation of 70 to 80 people regularly attending this earlier service. Again there was a reluctance to end it, but we did, perhaps unwisely.

At the end of a third period we decided to run the early service every Sunday morning of the year, and have done so ever since. The church has grown and it has become impossible to bring the two congregations together under the same roof at the same time. We learned valuable lessons about planting a second congregation. In the past the church had planted two other churches. This time, planting another congregation, using the same facilities, was a new experience.

Having grown numerically, we are committed to maintaining

the health of the church and creating opportunities for every member to grow spiritually. We are committed to local and world mission, continuing to support church members working overseas and in the UK. We want to see God add to the church daily those who are being saved.

How do we go about this?

Just as an aircraft pilot must first be committed to the idea of flying before he or she learns to fly, in the same way a congregation must be committed to the belief that God wants his church to grow in quality and quantity. Rick Warren, Pastor of Saddleback Community Church in southern California, helpfully describes five different levels of people groups within every community:

> The *Community* – Those living around the church.
> The *Crowd* – Those who attend regularly, but are not members.
> The *Congregation* – Those who are committed Christians and members.
> The *Committed* – Those members who are serious about growing to spiritual maturity.
> The *Core* – Those members who are actively serving in ministry in the church, the community, and the world.
> *The task in any sized church is to move people from the community to the core.*[9]

We are committed to this task. The first step was to make the church attractive and relevant to the community without compromising the gospel. Not long after we completed the extensive building alterations and established the second morning service, the church faced a further challenge. The pizza restaurant adjacent to the church building went on sale. This was an opportunity for the church to add extra, needed accommoda-

---

[9] Rick Warren, *The Purpose-Driven Church*, Zondervan 1995, p. 153.

tion and provide a further bridge to the community. The church was challenged to pray and give. If the amount of money needed to buy the property was given or promised within the two-month period during which we had the option to purchase, we would go ahead. We did, with a strong sense that 'It seemed good to the Holy Spirit and to us' (Acts 15:28). We changed the pizza restaurant into a coffee shop, disappointingly for some, but this has proved a great opportunity for ministry and bridge-building with the community.

Three times in nine years the church has broadcast its morning services live on the ITV network and once on BBC Radio 4, plus on a number of other occasions on regional ITV and Channel Four. The opportunities presented to us have been unusual. On three other occasions the Sunday morning service was broadcast on the ITV network, having been pre-recorded. The last networked full Sunday worship service of the old millennium was from Frinton Free Church, and the first networked full Sunday worship service of the new millennium was from the church, on 2nd January 2000.

In 1999 the church took the next step towards enabling growth to continue. We wanted to offer worship to God that was worthy of his character and relevant and attractive to the unchurched community. We wanted to increase the effectiveness of our weekday ministry to both the churched and unchurched, to children and youth and people of all ages. Once again, after a sustained period of prayer, fasting and giving, the church decided to make whatever alterations to the building were necessary to allow and encourage the spiritual health and growth of the church. Another property adjacent to the church was purchased. The future may include starting further congregations and planting new ones in other parts of the town. Some 15,000 people live within 15 minutes of our church, and along with the other churches of the town, we long to see those people incorporated into the family of God and growing in their relationship with him.

All growth is painful, and Frinton Free Church has experienced growing pains throughout its history. However, the
opportunities for ministry and mission that God has sent us
have been full of potential, if also demanding. As Rick Warren
writes:

> Believe me, it is an incredibly difficult task to lead people from self-
> centred consumerism to being servant-hearted Christians. It is not
> a task for fainthearted ministers or those who don't like to get their
> religious robes wrinkled. But it is what the Great Commission is all
> about.[10]

The search for people

The key issue is relevancy. The chief reason why people stop
going to church, or don't even start in the first place, is its lack
of relevance. Throughout the twentieth century churches have
changed to try to maintain relevant contact with the community. As we have seen in one church, early in the twentieth
century, the Sunday evening worship service was considered to
be the main point of entry for the unchurched. During the
1960s and 1970s, the emphasis changed to Sunday mornings.
Then, another change took place when afternoon Sunday
schools were transferred to Sunday mornings and were run par-
allel to the morning service. This triggered the introduction of
family-based services. The Sunday morning worship service in
most churches now draws a much larger congregation than the
evening, and in many places the evening service has been dis-
continued altogether.

Another change began when the midweek activities became
the primary contact point with non-Christians. For many
people the first experience of church happened in a parents
and toddlers group, a pre-school playgroup, a coffee shop, a

---

[10] Rick Warren, *The Purpose-Driven Church*, p. 46.

support group, a weekend retreat, a wedding, a funeral, or some other weekday activity. If the midweek event is a positive experience, the newcomer might risk venturing into church on a Sunday.

At Frinton Free Church we have used a number of special bridge-building events to complement our weekday activities. For example, in 1998 we showed key World Cup football matches live on a large TV screen in the social rooms belonging to the local tennis club. This drew hundreds of unchurched people alongside Christians. The common focus of World Cup football broke down barriers and opened the way for conversations about faith. It also created interest in our church. There were opportunities for public stories of faith, such as from former Football League referee, Peter Foakes, who had recently become a committed Christian and church member. During late-night shopping prior to Christmas, we threw a Christmas party for the whole main street, drawing hundreds to a variety of events ranging from traditional carol singing to a video wall, live bands, a live nativity scene, a colourfully decorated church, and free hot dogs, cokes, coffee and mince pies for anyone who came along. Church, which has so often had the reputation of asking either for money or for people to come to church, was here simply giving a party for the whole community. As a bridge-builder, it worked. It helped to create confidence in the church and showed it to be welcoming and alive to non-church-goers. Significant conversations took place. As a result people have come to faith who first came to church at a Christmas event. These kinds of events are used to help build community confidence in the church and are part of the process of evangelism.

We have also had bridge-building events among children and youth. We try for at least three such events a year. One is a 'church swim' when everyone is invited to the leisure centre swimming pool which the church takes over for a few hours. This draws people from all age groups. A 'bouncy castle' and a 'treasure hunt' are simple ideas which are some children's only experience of 'church'. Such events enable parents to meet leaders and unchurched parents to meet Christian parents. These special events have been effective in building community confidence, attracting people to church, and building one-to-one relationships.

In the 1990s many churches attempted to attract new people into church through 'seeker services'. These were not always successful, because churches often lacked the skills, expertise and equipment to make them effective. In many instances, evidence shows that seeker services have appealed more to the formerly churched than to the unchurched, and the formerly churched haven't always liked the changes. There is more about this approach in later chapters.

According to Christian Research, Britain is still a religious nation. In 1995, the number of people claiming to be Christians stood at 42.2 million, compared with 42.3 million 20 years before.[11]

The point is, there is still a window of opportunity to reach our nation for Christ through the local church. The challenge to the Christian is still to 'go and make disciples'. The invitation that we carry to the unchurched is to 'come' into the family of God. Such a challenge and invitation has radical but thrilling implications for the church of the twenty-first century. We have to apply the power that makes it happen, and unleash the potential of the local church.

[11] *UK Christian Handbook 1997*, 'Religious Trends'.

3

A Journey into Ministry

An elderly, retired minister tapped me on the shoulder and asked: 'Isn't it time you thought about going into the ministry?' He had no idea that I had felt God's call to ministry a couple of years earlier. Neither did he know that I had been fighting against the idea for several months. At the age of 18 I had an overwhelming conviction that God was calling me, but I kept it to myself for two good reasons. One, I didn't particularly like the idea, and two, I was frightened of people's reactions. The first few years of my life had been dominated by my stepfather, whose violent abuses left me with very little self-esteem and a complete lack of confidence. I left school at 15 without a single qualification, a very unlikely candidate for ministry.

God began to work in my life. He gave me sufficient confidence to start preaching and I knew then that I was on a journey. When I was 22 years old Spurgeon's Theological College, London, accepted me to begin training for the Baptist ministry.

The day before going to Spurgeon's, I had serious doubts. I called the minister of my home church and said, 'I don't believe this is right.' He asked, 'Why not?' 'Because I believe God has called me to be an evangelist, and I can do that by staying in my job and preaching whenever the opportunity comes,' I said. The truth is, it was an excuse. I disliked the idea of going to college for four years. I was trying desperately to get out of it as I was terrified of academic study. The Revd Hubert Janisch saw through my feeble attempt to avoid God's purpose for my life. I was not prepared for the loving but forceful rebuke he gave me, but he was right: my ministry was to be rooted in the local church.

'I don't think I should become the minister of a local church,' I said. 'I believe God has called me to be an evangelist.' This time it was Dr George Beasley-Murray, the college principal, who was the target of my efforts to avoid local church ministry. It was towards the end of the four-year college course when students found themselves negotiating settlements into churches.

'You won't last,' said George, who spotted another excuse for hard work and my aspirations to become the next Billy Graham! 'If you are called to evangelism, you must do what Spurgeon did. Evangelize from a local church. Have a local church behind you. Without that, you may not have much of a ministry.' I have never forgotten those words.

Effective evangelism occurs through the local church

I began my ministry as a theological student in a small church of about 50 members. Two things happened during the 18 months I served as a student pastor. I met the church secretary's daughter who later became my wife, Dorothy. And the church grew spiritually and numerically, but not without a deacon severely reprimanding me for reading from a modern translation of the Bible and taking away a key worker from the church!

After leaving Spurgeon's College we moved from a church of less than a hundred members to one of three thousand. For the next 12 months I served as the associate minister of a large Baptist church in Louisville, Kentucky. I also enrolled as a special student at the Southern Baptist Theological Seminary in Louisville. This proved to be a very formative year in my ministry. I served under the leadership of Dr Lewis Drummond, who later became an associate evangelist with Billy Graham and Professor of Evangelism and Church Growth at Beeson Divinity School, Samford University, Birmingham, Alabama.

During that year I learned many principles of church health and growth that have remained with me. I also realized how much British Christians had contributed to the North American scene. The Americans viewed our history with high regard. I admired their vision for evangelism, their faith for growth, their ability to communicate, and their strategy for developing different forms of ministry, some of which we are only just beginning in the UK.

During the past 30 years I have visited the USA on numerous occasions. I have preached in hundreds of churches in Canada and across America. I have closely studied many of those churches in both rural and inner city settings. I have also watched with interest how many, especially young, people in Britain have adopted aspects of the American lifestyle without really knowing it. Business corporations, the media, sports and leisure, shopping, banking, aviation, entertainment, many living patterns, have steadily followed the American lead. That doesn't mean we necessarily welcome these new patterns, but it does mean that our twenty-first century lifestyle, along with other Western nations, is being impacted by America.

There are principles to learn from many American churches if we are to reach twenty-first century UK culture. However, a word of caution is needed. Some British church leaders travel to America and form conclusions about large American churches without understanding the American culture, and overlooking the fact that 95 per cent of American churches have fewer than 250 members. What works there may or may not work in the UK. We need to take a closer look at some of America's smaller churches as well as the mega-churches. Some pastors and lay leaders have attended big conferences at the Crystal Cathedral in Los Angeles, Willow Creek in Chicago, or similar places, and then tried to apply some inappropriate methods to our churches only to find that they don't always work. We have to know the culture from which these ideas come, as well as understand and adapt them to our own.

We can also learn principles for growing healthy and balanced churches from other parts of the world such as South America, Africa, Asia and Eastern Europe. During visits to Romania and Albania, for example, I have realized that churches there have much to teach us.

The basics

A student pilot soon learns that every airfield is surrounded by a rectangle of invisible flight paths made up of four sections, or legs. The direction in which the aircraft takes off is the *upwind leg*. The aircraft climbs to a specified height and makes a 90-degree right- or left-hand turn on to the *crosswind leg*. Continuing to climb, the pilot later makes another 90-degree turn which brings the aircraft on to the *downwind leg*, travelling in the opposite direction from which it took off. Now flying straight and level for a while the next 90-degree turn in the rectangle brings the aircraft on to the *base leg*. The last turn and the aircraft is on final approach, preparing to land, flying once more on the upwind leg of the airport circuit or pattern. Every pilot must practise this flight pattern until it becomes second nature. In a similar way, I have discovered the benefits of following four biblical principles of church health until they became second nature in my ministry. These are as follows:

- Preach a positive message.
- Prepare people for effective ministry.
- Pray and plan for growth.
- Practise the purpose of the church.

I have followed these four basic principles in each of the churches I have served. These churches varied in size, had their own ethos and identity, and were in different parts of the UK. One started as a church of 70 members in the industrial Midlands. One was in a town centre, in a multi-racial setting in an economically deprived area. Another was in a middle-class commuter town on the edge of a very mixed housing estate. Frinton Free Church is in a mixed community in the centre of a small Essex town. Each church grew as a result of these four principles. This has been particularly true in the Frinton congregation.

After 30 years in ministry, I have discovered that what makes the difference between a growing church and a non-growing church is whether or not these four principles are incorporated into its life. Often they are there but not identified. Where they are identified and consciously implemented and encouraged, spiritual and numerical growth does take place.

Each of these four principles needs unpacking. Behind them are numerous other principles, but these provide a starting place to change attitudes in a local church. It is not my prerogative to tell any church how to operate, but I offer these tried and tested principles in the hope that they can be applied in situations where the tide of decline can be turned and growth can begin to take place.

These principles apply to churches of any size. My own experience is that leading a church of 50 members is very different from leading a church of 500, but the basic principles of spiritual and numerical growth are the same. We need churches of every size. There are many things that only a small church can do. And there are many things that only a larger church can do. We need both to make an impact on our nation. But whether your congregation is large or small right now, I am convinced that God doesn't want you to be satisfied with a church that never grows.

Some local churches struggle to survive, and faithful and

loyal pastors, often unpaid and unrewarded, work loyally and uncomplainingly. Wherever God has called us we must challenge our members to 'go', and then to invite people to 'come' into the family of God. We cannot emphasize the 'going' to the exclusion of the 'coming'. We need both.

I identify with those who say as Rick Warren does:

> I love the church of Jesus Christ with all my heart. Despite all its faults (due to our sinfulness) it is still the most magnificent concept ever created. It has been God's chosen instrument of blessing for two thousand years. It has survived persistent abuse, horrifying persecution, and widespread neglect. Parachurch organisations and other Christian groups come and go, but the church will last for eternity. It is worth giving our lives for and it deserves the best.[1]

In 1998 the Fanfare Project was launched with the backing of the Archbishop of Canterbury, Dr George Carey, Cardinal Basil Hume, the Roman Catholic leader in the UK, and the other leaders of mainstream denominations. It was presented by Steve Chalke, my former associate pastor for four years. It set out ten 'practical goals' for churches at the beginning of the twenty-first century that echo the purpose of this book. People have criticized them for being simplistic, yet there are literally thousands of churches that are not doing these simple things that can make such a difference:

1. We will make you welcome.
2. We will be family friendly.
3. We will make sure you can hear clearly.
4. We will be practical and relevant.
5. We will help you explore answers to your deepest questions.
6. We will offer you time to stop and think in a busy life.
7. We will help you make sense of the Bible and who Jesus is.

---

[1] Rick Warren, *The Purpose-Driven Church*, Zondervan 1995, p. 21.

8. We will make sure your visit will be helpful but challenging.
9. We will help you discover for yourself God's love, acceptance and forgiveness.
10. We will offer you the chance to make a new start.

The Holy Spirit is moving churches to rethink what they are doing, and it is my hope that the remaining chapters of this book will contribute to the achievement of these goals. God's Spirit is moving powerfully in many parts of the world, in different ways, in different cultures. Perhaps in the UK it is time for us to address these very practical issues.

Preach a Positive Message

4

Be Committed to Your Message

Preaching a positive message involves more than the Sunday sermons. We need to assess the church's entire presence in the community, its buildings, ministry, worship, fellowship and attitude. The whole church needs to be a positive statement about the kingdom of God, but let's start with the sermon. Boring and irrelevant sermons are one of the main causes for declining church attendance.

4.1 A message to change as well as inform

Every pilot on the threshold of the runway must have faith that his aircraft can fly. The pilot must be completely committed both to the idea of flying and to the belief that the machine is designed to rise into the air. In the same way the church must be totally dedicated to its message, believing that the gospel has the power to change and transform people's lives. This is the point of 'take-off' in any healthy church. Unless we are totally committed to the positive effects of the gospel we shall never get off the ground.

The gospel offers hope, purpose, direction, fulfilment, peace, something worth living for, principles and values to live by, acceptance and affirmation. The fundamental message of the

Bible is one of hope. We proclaim the God of hope through telling the stories of people in the Bible. We show through both Old and New Testaments that God does not always take us out of the crises of life, but is with us in them and can bring us through them. People respond to such hope as long as it's not contrived.

Psalm 103 talks about 'benefits'. 'Praise the Lord, O my soul, and forget not all his benefits.' The author lists those 'benefits': 'He forgives all my sins and heals all my diseases; he redeems my life from the pit and crowns me with love and compassion. He satisfies my desires with good things, so that my youth is renewed like the eagle's.' 'The Lord is compassionate and gracious, slow to anger and abounding in love.' 'He does not treat us as our sins deserve or repay us according to our iniquities. For as high as the heavens are above the earth, so great is his love for those who fear him; as far as the east is from the west, so far has he removed our transgressions from us.' Throughout the psalm, the psalmist continues reciting the 'benefits' of knowing God.

When Jesus stood up in the synagogue in Nazareth and announced his mission, he made positive statements. He quoted from Isaiah, and every statement proclaimed the good news, and benefits of his ministry: 'good news to the poor'; 'freedom for the prisoners'; 'recovery of sight for the blind'; 'to release the oppressed'; 'to proclaim the year of the Lord's favour' (Luke 4:18–19). The gospel is essentially good news. Even repentance can be preached in a positive way: turning from darkness to light; from blindness to sight; from lost to being found; from death to life.

Some preachers seem to emphasize what the Bible is against rather than the hope it embraces. It's what Rick Warren calls '"Ain't it awful!" preaching. . . . It is long on diagnosis and short on remedy. It rarely changes anything. Instead of lighting a candle, it just curses the darkness.'

As a religious advisor to one of the ITV companies and part of the *Morning Worship* team for the ITV network, and currently the *Sunday Morning* programme, one of my frequent responsibilities has been to read sermon manuscripts submitted by preachers for television. I am amazed how many sermons begin, and in some cases continue, negatively. The preachers have approximately eight minutes of television time in which to reach the largest congregation any clergyman in the UK is likely to have in the whole of their lifetime, yet often the message is phrased in negative terms.

Preaching a positive message is not the same as compromising the message. Jesus preached repentance in a positive way, but never compromised the truth. Mark tells us at the beginning of his Gospel: 'Jesus went into Galilee, proclaiming the good news of God. "The time has come," he said. "The kingdom of God is near. Repent and believe the good news!"' (Mark 1:14–15).

John Chrysostom (AD 347–407), known as 'golden mouth', was a man regarded by many as one of the greatest preachers in the history of the church. He built his preaching on five principles:[1]

- An excellent knowledge of the Bible.
- A good command of language.
- A compassionate heart for people.
- An ability to relate theology to everyday life.
- A passionate enthusiasm when preaching.

4.2 An excellent knowledge of the Bible

The authority and centrality of the Bible cannot be compromised in preaching that is persuasive and life-changing. When the truth of the Bible is related to human needs, people become interested. Martin Robinson, the director of mission and theology at the Bible Society in the UK, said:

---

[1] *Baptist Leader*, no. 14 (summer 1996).

It has taken many decades for the Bible to become a closed book, and we should not imagine that it will be reopened quickly. But if tomorrow is to be filled with genuine hope, then the Bible must be open to all, however long it might take.

Preachers can no longer take the biblical knowledge of their congregations for granted.

The purpose of the Bible is clearly set out in 2 Timothy 3:16, 'All scripture is God-breathed and is useful for teaching, rebuking, correcting and training in righteousness, so that the man of God may be thoroughly equipped for every good work.'

The word of God is powerful in the hands of the Holy Spirit. It produces faith on the part of hearers. It becomes a source of guidance, wisdom, assurance, and hope for the future. It encourages, comforts and challenges. It transforms lives and builds people up in their relationship with God and with others.

For several decades in the twentieth century, the evangelist Billy Graham was known for his familiar phrase 'The Bible says'. His conviction that he could trust the integrity of the Bible led him to say just before his famous London Crusades in the 1950s:

> I am going to present a God who matters, and who makes claims on the human race. He is a God of love, grace and mercy, but also a God of judgement. When we break his moral laws we suffer; when we keep them, we have inward peace and joy. I am going to insist that honesty and integrity pay in individual lives. I am calling for a revival that will cause men and women to return to their offices and shops to live out the teaching of Christ in their daily relationships. I am going to preach a gospel not of despair but of hope – hope for the individual, for society and for the world.[2]

History shows that during times of authentic spiritual revival, the Bible's message changes the lives of many people.

---

[2] John Pollock, *Billy Graham*, McGraw-Hill 1966, p. 118.

The Bible continues to capture the imaginations of film producers, television directors and music writers. If it excites preachers, it will captivate congregations as well. Yet sometimes we have turned the most exciting, positive and relevant book in the world into tedious talk. Rick Warren points out that 'When God's word is taught in an uninteresting way, people don't just think the pastor is boring, they think God is boring! We slander God's character if we preach with an uninspiring style or tone.'[3]

Churches have different approaches to teaching the Bible. Some preachers emphasize verse-by-verse expository preaching, while others work steadily through a whole book of the Bible over several Sundays. Some take on topical series, others follow a lectionary designed for the Christian year. Whatever our method, the important principle is to explain the Bible so that its message becomes understood, relevant and clear.

Roy Clements, in the *Cambridge Papers*, writes about 'expository preaching in a postmodern world'. He argues that it still has a place in a postmodern culture:

> While the style of preaching may well have to be radically revised if it is to communicate effectively in our contemporary world, the expository method must continue to inform the public teaching of any church which wishes to remain securely biblical in its ethos.[4]

Preaching sermons in series and in a consistent style helps to build people up. The congregation knows what to expect week by week, and if the message connects with people where they are, then they are more likely to return and encourage others to come with them. There are numerous churches that have demonstrated how this approach builds a congregation week by week, and almost service by service. Tell people on Sunday

---

[3] Rick Warren, *The Purpose-Driven Church*, Zondervan 1995, p. 231.
[4] *Cambridge Papers*, vol. 7, no. 3 (September 1998).

mornings what is going to be preached in the evening, or the next Sunday morning, and if it is compellingly relevant, we have clear evidence that congregations grow.

In the New Testament, Philip explained to the Ethiopian a section of the Old Testament book of Isaiah. The story makes it clear that it's not enough to read Scripture; it needs someone to explain it. 'How can I understand what I am reading, unless someone explains it to me?' Then comes a statement that challenges every preacher: 'Then Philip began with that very passage of Scripture and told him the good news about Jesus' (Acts 8:35). Philip employed another principle, one that Jesus always used: starting where people are, with what they are interested in, addressing their need, what is important to them, and what questions they are asking.

In order to reopen the Bible, as Martin Robinson puts it, we also need to make the Bible accessible. There is no need to read long, complicated passages in order to preach from them. Read something simple to understand, but relevant to the day's message, and explain the more complex passage in the course of the sermon. Needless to say, it also helps to read from one of the newer translations of the Bible.

Pew Bibles make it possible for the page number to be announced. The argument that this discourages people from bringing their own Bible to church is far outweighed by the number of people who don't bring a Bible to church anyway, either because they feel embarrassed trying to find the passage that's being read, or simply because they do not have a Bible. Unchurched members of the congregation need practical support to become familiar with the Bible.

4.3 A good command of language

This is the second of Chrysostom's principles. Jesus spoke in an attractive manner. The people heard him gladly. 'The large crowd listened to him with delight' (Mark 12:37).

Most surveys show that the chief reason why people don't attend church is because they consider the preaching boring. Leith Anderson writes: 'Leaders must be attuned to their culture. It is not enough to know the Bible. We must also know our culture and our people.'[5] He goes on to point out that congregations include growing numbers of biblically illiterate people, so suggests using sermon titles and language more familiar to the unchurched: 'Titling a sermon on Luke 18:18–27 "The Guy Who Had Everything and Still Wasn't Satisfied," rather than "The Rich Young Ruler," doesn't make the sermon any less biblical. It makes it more relevant.'[6]

Preachers need to work hard on their language. It is so easy to slip into a sort of holy-speak. Three mistakes are commonly made. The first is speaking in theological terms that are familiar to mature believers but not necessarily to younger believers or the unchurched. It's a little like using complex medical terms to a patient, or aviation terminology to a passenger, or film and television jargon to someone who simply wants to watch a film. After John Wesley wrote a sermon, he read it to his maid and then took out any words she didn't understand. The problem is that it's far easier for theologically trained clergy to speak in theological terms than it is to interpret theology into everyday language. We need to take to heart the words of Jesus in John 12:49 – 'the Father who sent me commanded me what to say and *how* to say it'. Jesus had no time for spin doctors, but he did recognize the importance not only of *what* to say but *how* to say it. Speak out a sermon to yourself before preaching it to others. What writes well or is well thought out may not necessarily speak well. Sermons are heard, not read.

A second mistake is to think we are using everyday language

---

[5] Leith Anderson, *A Church for the Twenty-First Century*, Bethany House 1992, p. 63.
[6] *Ibid.*, p. 205.

when in reality we are using language from the past. For example, I once heard a preacher describing the storm on Galilee. He wasn't using any long words, but the words he used were out of date. He said 'when the storm arose' and I wondered how a newsreader would report such an event. Probably something like 'when the storm broke', or 'when the storm hit'. The disciples 'cry to him in their distress and their cry goes unheeded'. The disciples were pleading for help. 'At the heart of the gospel is a message about God's identification with our human condition in the life and death of Jesus.' Put that in everyday language!

A third mistake is to use only one particular style of preaching. I know from personal experience that television has changed the rules of communication. It has shortened most people's attention span. It has caused them to have higher expectations of communication. Television bombards people with masses of information, so they are more selective in what they choose to hear. One of Gatwick Airport's Terminal Duty Managers explained why they don't make flight departure announcements any more. 'If you have to make a lot of announcements over the PA, passengers go what we call "PA deaf" and simply don't hear them.' Some people in our congregations have become 'sermon deaf' because the style and language is too familiar. Different sermon content often calls for different styles and language.

4.4 A compassionate heart for people

'It is doubtful that there is anything more basic, more Christlike, and therefore more Christian than compassion.'[7] All too often sermons will beat up rather than lift up. Some hardened evangelical churchgoers don't think they have been to church unless they have been castigated for their lack of com-

---

[7] Chuck Swindoll, *Compassion*, Word Books 1984, p. 39.

mitment. But the mood is changing. Today's people come to church looking for inspiration, motivation, renewal of spirit and refreshment of mind; to be lifted up rather than beaten down.

In most congregations there are emotionally bruised and hurting people. Some have had a tough week and they are wondering how they can face the next. Churches should be places where broken lives can be put back together, where lost people can find purpose and meaning through faith in Christ. In many congregations there are people who are bereaved; people struggling with ill health; people struggling with tense relationships, either at home or in the workplace; people who are facing pressures and tensions of many different kinds, trying to come to terms with issues of sexuality, finance, parenthood, loneliness, guilt, addictions, and all kinds of relational problems.

As a young minister I remember a businessman telling me there were two ways to make a donkey move forward. One was with the offer of a carrot, and the other was with a sharp smack on its rear. The implication was clear. Most of my preaching was a kick from behind. The eerie thing was, people seemed to like it! But then I made another discovery. I realized one day that by preaching practical messages of hope, people were not simply listening, they were entering into the sermon and beginning to share it with me. Ephesians 4:29 says: 'Do not let any unwholesome talk come out of your mouths, but only what is helpful for building others up according to their needs . . .'

Congregations instinctively know when a preacher is speaking from the heart and personal experience. Congregations identify with preachers when they share something of their own spiritual journey, or their own pressures. Let people know that you understand their struggles. We feel God is much closer to us when we read Hebrews 4:15 – 'we do not have a high priest who is unable to sympathise with our weaknesses, but we have one who has been tempted in every way, just as we are – yet was without sin. Let us then approach the throne of grace with confidence, so that we may receive mercy and find grace to help us in our time of need.'

G. Campbell Morgan, a famous preacher earlier in the twentieth century, really understood the needs of his generation:

> He once listened to an articulate young preacher as he delivered his sermon. A bystander later asked him for his evaluation of the preacher and the sermon. Morgan answered, 'He is a very good preacher and when he has suffered he will be a great preacher.'[8]

Matthew 9:36 reminds us, 'When he saw the crowds, he had compassion on them, because they were harassed and helpless.' Later in chapter 14, verse 14, 'When Jesus landed and saw a large crowd, he had compassion on them.' The compassion of Jesus permeates the Gospels. The people sensed it as he moved among them. A preacher who has a compassionate heart for people will know their hurts, pains, fears and hopes. Chuck Swindoll says: 'Others will not care how much we know until they know how much we care.' The Holy Spirit uses compassionate, sensitive preaching to touch the lives of people.

4.5 An ability to relate theology to everyday life

This is the fourth of Chrysostom's principles. Remember how Jesus announced his ministry, quoting from Isaiah: 'good news to the poor'; 'freedom for the prisoners'; 'recovery of sight for the blind'; 'to release the oppressed'; 'to proclaim the year of the Lord's favour' (Luke 4:18–19). Jesus later invites people to 'Come to me, all you who are weary and burdened, and I will give you rest' (Matthew 11:28). What an offer! Following Christ means self-denial and cross-bearing on a daily basis, but in the

---

[8] Anderson, *A Church for the Twenty-First Century*, p. 203.

positive context of God's support. 'For whoever wants to save his life will lose it, but whoever loses his life for me and for the gospel will save it' (Mark 8:35).

On the day of Pentecost, Peter and the disciples preached good news. In answer to the crowd's question 'What shall we do?' Peter replied, 'Repent and be baptised, every one of you, in the name of Jesus Christ so that your sins may be forgiven. And you will receive the gift of the Holy Spirit' (Acts 2:37–8). You won't find a better offer anywhere.

Relating the Bible to everyday life is a big challenge for any church. Phillips Brookes, famous for writing the Christmas hymn 'O little town of Bethlehem', wrote a memorable book called *Lectures on Preaching*. In it he defines preaching as 'truth through personality'. He pleads with preachers to open one side of their lives to the truth of God, and the other side to the vast needs of men and women. Then, he says, bring the truth of God to meet the needs of men and women. Paul describes Christians as 'ministers of reconciliation' trusted with the 'message of reconciliation' (2 Corinthians 5:18–19).

Research by Mark Greene, a former vice-principal of the London Bible College, suggests that one in two preachers lacked relevance, even though a sermon was considered 'excellent' by congregations.

> The yearning for relevance was not accompanied by any significant level of complaint about the teaching of the Bible. Exegesis is not where people think the problem lies, though it is almost certainly an issue. In fact, most felt that the Bible was being taught, even if many felt it wasn't being applied. Indeed, it was clear that for some it was possible for someone to deliver an 'excellent' sermon that made no connection with their life.
>
> We've been strong on calling for the need to expound the text but less strong on answering people's questions – which is why 50% of evangelicals have never heard a sermon on work. . . . I think it's vital to tackle the Bible book by book, but it's not the only answer. At Pentecost, for example, Peter wasn't preaching on Joel because it

was the lectionary reading for the week but because he was being asked a question about grown people who appeared to be slewed out of their minds.[9]

Calvin Miller, a highly respected preacher in the USA, talks about 'marketplace preaching' – reaching people where they are. 'I have discovered', he says, 'that to grow a church from ten members to 3,500 members, you have to be able to start where the people are.' He calls for preaching that is relational, colloquial and relevant.

Rick Warren says boldly:

Preaching to felt needs is scorned and criticised in some circles as a cheapening of the Gospel and a sellout to consumerism. I want to state this in the clearest way possible: Beginning a message with people's felt needs is more than a marketing tool! It is based on the theological fact that God chooses to reveal himself to man according to our needs! Both the Old and New Testaments are filled with examples of this.[10]

I don't believe this means we are to preach a gospel of prosperity and success. Preaching that is all success-orientated and continually upbeat turns many people away. But people are hungry for good news that is earthed in reality. I used to believe it was enough to preach biblical principles and let the congregation work those out for themselves in their everyday lives. That might have been possible even a few decades ago. Today, people are looking for help. Application of the message is essential, sometimes offering additional help through people being available to talk to when the worship concludes, or suggesting further books to read or groups to attend. Relating theology to everyday life is what is called 'application'. I believe this is one

[9] Mark Greene, *The Three-Eared Preacher*, quoted in *Quadrant*, November 1998, published by Christian Research.

[10] Warren, *The Purpose-Driven Church*, p. 295.

of the most neglected areas of proclamation in British churches. We have been strong on exposition and weak on application.

Preaching has a similar role to public broadcasting. Both try to prepare people for the future:

> Broadcasting has a role in preparing and training people to come to terms with new ideas and visions: new technologies like computers, e-mail, the Internet; facing the fears and opportunities of new medical practices; questioning new political realities of Europe; new economics; the future needs for employment and unemployment, for wealth or poverty, for education and training.[11]

Preaching is equipping people for a future, both in this world and the next.

More than ever before the need for preaching to be practical and relevant, as well as biblical, is paramount. We should speak to the needs of the congregation in such a way that our preaching makes a difference to people's lives. Rick Warren says, 'Every week I begin with a need, hurt, or interest and then move on to what God has to say about it in his word.'[12] American preachers have always been better at this than their British counterparts, although they sometimes go too far and fill the entire sermon with application but very little content. The British, on the other hand, tend to spend too much time on history and doctrine. I wish I had understood years ago what I have come to know the hard way – how to apply the message. Rick Warren puts this need in a nutshell when he says, 'Tell them why; show them how.'

Much has been written about the move from deductive to inductive preaching. Fred Craddock, a professor of preaching and New Testament, was asked why he championed inductive

---

[11] Robert McLeish, Director of Robert McLeish Associates Management and Media Training Consultancy.
[12] Warren, *The Purpose-Driven Church*, p. 295.

biblical preaching so much. He explained that he was 'giving the listeners room to arrive at conclusions rather than concluding and then preaching on it'.

Inductive preaching is not to be confused with lack of application. Deductive preaching starts with a general truth, explains it, and moves to *particular* applications. Inductive preaching, or reasoning, starts with a need or experience, moves on to the general truth and *then applies it* in a way that enables the listeners to make the sermon their sermon and draw their conclusion. For example, an inductive sermon may start with people's need for love, provide stories and examples of God's love in people's lives, state that God demonstrated love when he sent Jesus, and so reach the conclusion that 'God is love'. This is not to say that one style is right and the other wrong. They are just different and one style might be more appropriate for a specific congregation than another.

One style focuses more on telling the congregation what to do, using parental words such as 'ought', 'should', and 'must'. The other style explains the issues, presents the alternatives, and then seeks to persuade, but leaves the decision up to the listener.

The Bible, and the New Testament in particular, was written to help people with specific problems and needs. Our preaching should also always be concerned with addressing the real needs in people's lives, addressing the issues and current concerns that people share.

Teaching Bible knowledge alone can achieve little. Although it may be truth, at that moment it may be irrelevant truth to the listeners. Something can be true but at the same time irrelevant. One of the mistakes often made is to overload listeners with information about the biblical text. My former associate pastor, Steve Chalke, now a broadcaster and Founding Director of Oasis Trust, wrote:

The previous week had been difficult. As I sat in my pew that Sunday morning, I was at my wits' end. But rather than providing the help that I so desperately needed, the sermon – which dealt in some depth with the three Hebrew words for 'worship' used in one of the Psalms – only multiplied my frustration and despair. I left the building after the service, praying, with all the sarcasm I could muster, 'Well thanks God! I'm really struggling to be a sensitive husband, wise father, good boss, loyal friend and responsible member of society. I can't say I've had much help in any of these areas, but at least I now have a better grasp of some Hebrew words for worship!'[13]

Steve goes on to say that positive preaching addresses human needs and issues with a clear, practical spirituality that ordinary people can understand, relate to and benefit from. 'So many sermons on so many Sundays in so many churches are theologically sound, exegetically precise and practically irrelevant.' Preaching needs to move from the issues and situations to the Bible. Doing it the other way round increases the danger of being abstract. We are reminded in 1 Corinthians 14:3 that 'everyone who prophesies speaks to men for their strengthening, encouragement and comfort'.

4.6 A passionate enthusiasm when preaching

Preaching should be done with energy, passion and enthusiasm. The potential effect of good content can be lost when the delivery is dull and lifeless. People are looking at the messenger as well as listening to the message. Is the messenger committed to his or her message? Does it come from their heart? Phillips Brooks, who (see above) defined preaching as 'truth through personality', wrote that

truth must come through the person, not merely over his lips, not merely into his understanding and out through his pen. It must

---

[13] Steve Chalke, *Backchat,* the Oasis newsletter, Autumn 1997.

come through his character, his affections, his whole intellectual and moral being.[14]

Don't try to be someone you are not. Be true to yourself and to your own convictions, but also be true to your text.

How often we have heard sections from the Bible which describe joy and hope read in a manner that conveys the opposite. Reading the Bible in an uninspired manner is being irresponsible to the congregation. The same principle applies to public praying, and to the sermon. Phillips Brooks makes the point that the sermon is a *message* of which we are *witnesses*.

> In these two words together, I think, we have the fundamental conception of the matter of all Christian preaching. It is to be a message given to us for transmission, but yet a message which we cannot transmit until it has entered into our own experience, and we can give our testimony of its spiritual power. The minister who keeps the word 'message' always written before him, as he prepares his sermon in the study, or utters from the pulpit, is saved from the tendency to wanton and wild speculation, and from the mere passion of originality. He who never forgets that word 'witness', is saved from the unreality of repeating by rote mere forms of statement which he has learned as orthodox, but never realised as true.[15]

If the messenger is gripped and excited by his message, then the congregation is more likely to be gripped and motivated by the message as well. In 2 Corinthians 5:19 we read that God 'has committed to us the message of reconciliation. We are therefore Christ's ambassadors, as though God were making his appeal through us – we implore you on Christ's behalf: Be reconciled to God.'

Preaching with a passionate enthusiasm doesn't mean we have to shout. With professional sound equipment in many

---

[14] Phillips Brooks, *Lectures on Preaching*, Allenson 1902, p. 8.
[15] *Ibid.*, pp. 14–15.

buildings preaching has developed into a more conversational style, but enthusiasm, passion and conviction must still be present. In Acts 2:40, Peter 'pleaded' with his hearers.

In the mid-nineteenth century some London churches were declining and preaching was considered by many to have out-lived its usefulness. But when the young Charles Spurgeon first preached at New Park Street Baptist Church in London

> the morning service ended and the impressed congregation – only eighty in number – filed out. That afternoon the good members fanned out over south London inviting friends to the evening service. A large congregation gathered in the evening.[16]

Charles Spurgeon soon began to build up the congregation spiritually and numerically and went on to preach to tens of thousands in the course of his ministry.

Preaching with passionate enthusiasm is not to be confused with preaching only what people want to hear. It is not a compromise of the gospel. It is a communication of the gospel in terms of what it is, 'good news'. When Jesus preached and taught, he dealt with all kinds of human need and conditions. He talked about money, food, clothing, forgiveness, fear, human relationships, and how to overcome all kinds of hang-ups and habits such as lying, cheating, destructive use of sex, prejudice, anger, hatred and murder. As the *News of the World* newspaper used to advertise itself, 'All human life is here'.

The primary goal of preaching is to change lives. The application of the sermon is to call for some form of commitment. Usually that is a process rather than a moment in time.

Being well prepared for preaching in the twenty-first century will mean far more than having three points and a poem. Sometimes there is too much theory and too little practicality.

---

[16] Lewis and Betty Drummond, writing on Susannah Spurgeon, *Women of Awakenings*, Kregel 1997, p. 147.

There needs to be a mix of theory and practice. Old sermons from previous years won't do. I constantly change my style and presentation, as it is important to stay fresh and relevant to *today's* needs.

Above all, let us preach a positive message. Phillips Brooks said:

> It has often seemed to me as if the vast amount of preaching which people hear must have one bad effect, in leaving on their minds a vague impression that this Christian life to which they are so continually urged must be a very difficult and complicated thing that it should take such a multitude of definitions to make it clear.[17]

4.7 Preaching in a postmodern age

Though few churches would use the word 'postmodern', many churches have been influenced by the postmodern age.

Postmodernism developed first among academics and artists and has quickly spread through our culture. At its most basic level, it refers to the passing of 'modernity' – the dominant worldview since the Enlightenment.

Modernity was supposed to provide answers not only to solve all our conflicts and problems, but for the whole human dilemma. However, at the end of the twentieth century, despite advancements in science, medicine and technology, people have realized that none of these accomplishments can save us from the evils that plague us. And so they have rejected modernity, and a postmodern age has come.

Postmodernism says there are no longer any absolute, objective truths. Distinctions are blurred between right and wrong, male and female, fantasy and reality. Heather Wraight of Christian Research has summed up the mood of the age by saying that people want 'Spirituality without Christianity; the

---

[17] Brooks, *Lectures on Preaching*, Allenson 1902, p. 2.

environment without the Creator; words without meaning; individuality without belonging; the present without a future'. This makes other faiths and lifestyles more acceptable than in the past.

Postmodernism means:

> Values in post-modern society have gone relative. We're told it's the end of a meta-narrative, the big explanation, the big Utopia. Instead you make up and write your own agenda.[18]

It is imperative the church understands the world in which it ministers. A growing church will not be a church locked in a time warp of the mid-twentieth century. Many churches have in fact seen the world pass them by because they have been more concerned with resisting change than reaching people for Christ.

However, we should avoid becoming too obsessed with relevance. Some churches in their desire to reach the culture have become like the culture. In the search for relevance they have lost the boldness to stand for truth.

> Modern culture is revolt against the truth, and postmodernism is but the latest form of this revolt. Ministry in these strange times calls for undiluted conviction and faithful apologetics. The temptations to compromise are great, and the opposition which comes to anyone who would claim to preach absolute and eternal truth is severe. But this is the task of the believing church.[19]

The biblical response to reaching a world for Christ is not cultural adaptation, but counter-cultural proclamation.

So how can the church today be an effective evangelist in a postmodern world? Our congregations and communities will

---

[18] Elaine Storkey, speaking at *Women in Mission* 1997, quoted in *Woman Alive*.
[19] Albert Mohler, President of Southern Seminary, Louisville, Kentucky.

not understand fully what is behind the moods and fancies of our day. However, they do know that we live in a very different spiritual and moral environment from previous generations, and that only a true spiritual revival will cut through it all. In the meantime, we can help our congregations to understand the world in which they minister, and to understand why they think and behave in the way they do. Coming to grips with the culture may be part of the preparation for true revival.

> The West appears to have said its definitive farewell to a Christian culture. Our secular colleagues are happy to recognise the debt our civilisation owes to the Christian faith to the extent that the faith, having been absorbed by culture itself, has become simply another cultural artifact. Christianity has become a historical factor subservient to a secular culture rather than functioning as the creative power it once was.[20]

Whatever may have been the case in the past, in today's culture the whole church needs to be involved in the process of evangelism. It cannot be left to mass crusades and special events of outreach. Evangelism is a process, and the whole church, day by day, week by week, and year by year, is to be involved. This is the purpose of the whole church, not just one group within it.

> As we approach the 21st Century, our obedience must be no less than that of the first-century church. We must proclaim and teach boldly the Word of God. We must be willing to take the gospel message into a culture that insists we keep our religion to ourselves. And we must let Scripture determine our methods and message rather than adjusting to the daily whims of culture.[21]

---

[20] Louis Dupre, Yale professor, quoted in *Christian Century* (July 1997), p. 654.
[21] Thom S. Rainer, *The Tie*, Southern Seminary, spring 1997, p. 12.

5

Create a Positive Environment

5.1 The right attitude

One of the most dangerous yet exhilarating sections of flight for a pilot comes soon after take-off. As the ground drops away and everything takes on a new perspective, the pilot gets the feeling of entering an entirely new world. But the pilot cannot relax and enjoy the scenery too much, for there is a lot to do. This is the time when the aircraft is most likely to stall. Although on full power, the angle of the aircraft is critical. Too steep an angle, and no matter how much power, the climb will come literally to a stop, before the aircraft plummets to the ground. Because the air speed over the control surfaces of the wings is much slower than when the aircraft is flying in a straight and level line, the controls become much less responsive. At this stage in the flight, two things are essential: power, and the 'attitude' of the aircraft. The angle of an aircraft in flight is always referred to as 'attitude'. I remember my instructor yelling at me, 'Watch your attitude! Watch your attitude!' I have heard that in other contexts too!

Perhaps our churches need someone to say to us over and over again, 'Watch your attitude! Watch your attitude!' 'Your attitude should be the same as that of Christ Jesus,' says Paul to the Christians at Philippi (Philippians 2:5). The servant attitude of Jesus is to be the servant attitude of the church.

A servant attitude is a positive attitude. Many people think that the church is always out to get something – usually money. Yet people like Zacchaeus (Luke 19), the Samaritan woman (John 4), and the crippled beggar (Acts 3), were all surprised that Jesus and the disciples wanted to give rather than to take. When the church gives to the community, through its worship and ministries, some people find it hard to believe there are no strings attached. They become more responsive when they encounter people with a servant attitude.

Years ago when someone came home from church they might have been asked: 'What was said?' Today, the question is more likely to be: 'What happened?' And if what happened was a positive experience, they are more likely to return, and even encourage someone else to go with them.

5.2 Become a missionary congregation

Christian truth and values can be portrayed negatively not only through sermons, but through unwelcoming buildings, by worship that caters only for the believer, and by the general attitude of the leaders and members. It doesn't matter whether a church is traditional or contemporary, charismatic or non-charismatic – any church can have a negative ethos.

Creating a positive environment and having a servant attitude is part of being a missionary congregation. The church sees the local community as a mission field just as needy as some parts of Africa or the Far East.

One of the statements by non-churchgoers in the book *The Search for Faith and the Witness of the Church* is

As for walking into a church, forget it! All those people murmuring! All that community singing stuff! It's years out of date. I live life in the fast lane. It doesn't fit my lifestyle. Maybe I'll want it when

I'm an OAP and start thinking about dying. But I can't belong to an outfit like your Church, no way![1]

Preaching a positive message includes creating a positive environment. It includes the environment in which the worship, teaching and weekday ministry takes place. It includes the vision and attitude of the leadership. It includes the spirit of the people. Surveys show that the main factor which contributes to a church's growth is an atmosphere of love among the membership. Such churches attract more people regardless of their theology, denomination or location. 'The beginning of the gospel about Jesus Christ, the Son of God' is how Mark's account of the life of Jesus begins. The Living Bible paraphrases that: 'Here begins the wonderful story of Jesus the Messiah, the Son of God' (Mark 1:1). So how do we create a positive environment that expresses this 'wonderful story'?

The physical, emotional and spiritual environment of the church becomes important because we are inviting people to a party! The parable of the great banquet in Luke 14 and Matthew 22 focuses on God's invitation to 'come' to what God has prepared. 'Come, for everything is now ready' (Luke 14:17). Jesus uses an invitation to a banquet as a sign of God's grace. In the parable the servants are commanded: 'Go out quickly into the streets and alleys of the town and bring in the poor, the crippled, the blind and the lame.'

There are two principles in the parable. One we have observed, the other we have neglected. Quite correctly we have encouraged believers to 'go' out into the world, but we have neglected the need to invite people to 'come' into the family of God – the church. In the parable everything was 'ready' for those who were to be invited. Often, our churches are not 'ready', and so we don't have the confidence, or see the

---

[1] *The Search for Faith and the Witness of the Church*, Church House Publishing 1996.

need, to invite people to come. Jesus tells the disciples to 'go' but with the clear command not just to tell people, but to 'make disciples . . . baptising them . . . teaching them' – in other words, to incorporate them into the family of God (Matthew 28:19–20). Because we have neglected to do this many local churches have become places for believers and not unbelievers, for the saved and not the sinners, for the found and not the lost, for the well and not the sick, for the healed and not the broken.

When the church gathers to worship, rejoice and celebrate, we meet as the family of God to connect with one another, to celebrate new life together, and to worship God. It feels great. All of us are present. And that's the problem. Then Jesus comes along and says: 'Don't get too satisfied. I care about the ones who are not here. The broken, the despairing, the lost, the grieving, the addicted, the abused, the bitter, the isolated and lonely, the poor, the rich, those who will find it hard to come into the kingdom of God; I want them in here but they are still out there, and many of them couldn't care less about my church.'

The church exists for those who are not yet in it, but all too often we want to keep it for ourselves. People shouted mockingly at Jesus, 'He saved others, but he can't save himself!' What they shouted was true. And as the principle was true for Jesus, so it is for his church. We cannot save ourselves if we would save others.

If we are faithful enough to 'go' out into all the world and invite people into the family of God, what we invite them into is all important.

5.3 The church is more than a building, but . . .

The building often creates a person's first impression of a church. The building can be either a negative or a positive presence in the community. Whether it is hundreds of years old or new, what it looks like creates a more powerful impression than what people hear in it. The building itself becomes a statement, a message, and is either positive or negative. It can convey life and relevance, or death and redundancy. Overgrown graveyards, out-of-date posters, buildings that have been neglected and are closed except for Sundays, all convey a negative message to the unchurched. Some Christians may argue that we are presenting a counter-culture to our materialistic, affluent society. However, that's not the message being received. We are perceived to be irrelevant.

Of course, the church is more than a building. It's people living every day by biblical standards and values in their homes, the workplace, and the world. The church is about relationships which are formed and strengthened by meeting in homes, by commitment to and caring for one another, by being accountable to one another, by growing together spiritually, by sharing in community projects, and relating to one another in the world of work. The church began with those who 'broke bread in their homes and ate together with glad and sincere hearts' (Acts 2:46). The first followers of Jesus allowed the word of God to govern and direct their everyday lives, dramatically transforming their attitudes, their goals and their relationships.

A building is not essential. Millions of churches all over the world begin their life without a building. But where a church does have its own premises, the building needs to be a positive statement of the Christian faith and message.

Facilities and physical environment have a lot to do with what happens in a service. The shape of your building will shape your service. Walk into some buildings and your mood will instantly brighten; walk into others and you'll feel depressed.[2]

---

[2] Rick Warren, *The Purpose-Driven Church*, Zondervan 1995, p. 264.

In my first pastorate in Coventry we began with a hall on a plot of ground. The hall was in daily use with the Boys' Brigade, pre-school playgroup, youth club, and various other activities. The same hall was used for worship services on Sunday. The small membership had remained fairly constant over the years. The Sunday morning service was more of a youth Bible study with very few adults in the congregation. There were plans to erect another building for worship, on the piece of ground next to the hall. I remember going from house to house in the neighbourhood inviting people to church. I will never forget their response. 'When you have a proper church, we'll come.' 'Do you have to wear a uniform to come to your church?' That was because the hall was associated with the Boys' Brigade. My assumption was that people were making excuses. However, a new octagonal church was built. The unusual construction caused interest, and when it opened, many of those who said they would attend did so! The original congregation doubled and then trebled. 'At last', some of them said, 'you're a church.'

In the UK one of the biggest problems facing churches is old, often inaccessible buildings. Some are maintained on a shoe-string by a faithful minority of worshippers. Some are so far past their use-by date that unless the congregation is relocated, the church will die. Indeed abandoned churches reinforce the impression that 'church' is now a thing of the past!

However, some churches have newer, more functional, multi-purpose premises. Some of these have a high level of weekday use. Pre-school playgroups, parents and toddlers groups, children's clubs, coffee mornings, or even coffee shops, luncheon clubs, youth activities and recreation activities make these buildings the centre of community life. They are accessible and visible. Even these, though, are sometimes allowed to be untidy and awkward for visitors on a Sunday.

There are 'warehouse' churches. There was a time when churches were being turned into warehouses. Now warehouses are being turned into churches. These buildings are often highly visible on easily accessible industrial estates, adaptable for multi-purposes, comparatively inexpensive to maintain, flexible and spacious. It can be argued that they lack aesthetic qualities and a total absence of ecclesiological or theological architecture or symbolism. We can imagine a class of children from a local school being shown around the building to be taught worship. 'There are no statues, Miss.' 'Which way do the people face, Miss?' 'Sir, why isn't there an altar?' Such symbols have been replaced by an array of musical instruments, public-address equipment, overhead projectors, screens, and colourful lighting.

The point is, buildings, if we have them, whether traditional or contemporary, are an important part of our message. Nothing is more negative and depressing than the sight of a church fronted by wrought-iron gates, padlocked with chains, in the middle of a rejuvenated town centre! Caring for our buildings so that they accomplish the purpose of the church is at the very least an expression of care, both for the church and the community in which it is placed.

Of course, in many cases, this is easier said than done. Some inner-city churches have a constant battle with vandalism. But the truth remains, buildings are either a help or a hindrance in reaching the community. Do as much as possible to make buildings a useful tool. There are some positive examples which show the value of good building facilities. Much has been made of the 'revival' at the Brownsville Assemblies of God Church in Pensacola, Florida from 1996 onwards. Thousands of people have come to faith through the ministry of that church. However, the leadership team and the members have had the benefit of excellent facilities in which to see their prayers answered. Although situated in a rather rundown part of the city, Brownsville has a splendid church complex. It has the benefit of ample parking space, a 2,300-seat sanctuary, and 1,200-seat chapel.

In Britain, the Clarendon Centre, Brighton, home of the Church of Christ the King, has a high-quality facility including a main auditorium seating over 1,000. It has been acoustically engineered for concerts and conferences, as well as for worship. This former warehouse has a spacious and welcoming foyer providing an excellent reception area. In addition there are five other rooms seating from 25 to 300 people. The home of King's Church in Eastbourne was a furniture warehouse. There is good parking, including bays for disabled persons. The main auditorium seats up to 1,000 people. A second hall seats up to 400. There are other smaller rooms, and again, a large foyer for reception with a bistro-style café seating approximately 50 to 60 people. There are also full kitchen facilities. Some churches are purpose built to provide a welcoming environment, attractive centres for worship, accessibility for people of all ages, with rooms and equipment for weekday ministry in the local community.

Providing a welcoming and non-threatening environment where people can worship is vital to the church's outreach to the community. For example, in Plymouth, an old vandalized pub, The Crown, has been transformed into a place where Christians can meet and worship and to which unchurched people can be invited. Adrian Hancock, writing about this former pub in the spring 1998 issue of *Church Growth Digest*, says: 'Attracting adults and making them feel comfortable on their own terms is important if they are ever to join the church and become worshippers, or even listen with an open mind to the Christian message.'

Buildings affect both churched and unchurched. Small congregations sometimes suffer from a lack of identity and low self-esteem due to their depressing buildings. So what can be done? This is often the steep climb towards getting off the ground. It is a highly sensitive and controversial area. It is at this point that a church often stalls. There is some hard work to be done.

5.4 Look at your building through a visitor's eyes

The regular congregation can get used to a cracked window or untidy vestibule. They hardly notice it any more. The outside of the building may be dirty and rundown. In particular, look at the entrance. Is it cold and dark, or is it light and welcoming? Some entrances to churches are so foreboding that it takes courage for even an occasional visitor from another church to enter, quite apart from an unchurched visitor. Look at the paintwork, the grounds, the noticeboards, and in the winter, the lighting.

Create a positive environment inside the church. Flowers and plants in the entrance and the church express life and colour. Use well-produced banners placed in strategic places. Change them before they get too dusty and familiar. In some churches the pulpit dominates the front, intimidating the worshipper. An untidy and cluttered platform area creates a 'don't care' attitude. Seating and temperature are also important; if there are pews, make them as comfortable as possible.

Sadly, some churches have corners, balconies, vestibules or other areas cluttered with old books, broken umbrellas, out-of-date notices, and dilapidated furniture that all says, 'We're out of date,' 'We're irrelevant,' 'We belong to a bygone age.'

At Frinton, we began looking at our buildings from a visitor's perspective. Our weekday entrance was dark and intimidating. It used to be behind a high hedge and wrought-iron gate, leading to a heavy door that opened into a tiny space leading to another heavy door. We did away with that in the late 1980s, but the entrance by today's standards was still dull and uninviting. The new scheme incorporated a wider, brighter, more welcoming entrance leading into a large reception space with easy access to the church, the coffee shop and other areas. Another entrance adjacent to a small car park, frequently used during weekday evenings, was even darker and more intimidating, particularly in winter. This was where many non-churchgoing parents collected their children from our weeknight children's activities. The waiting parents stood in the dull, dark-painted entrance. The main entrance to the church was overcrowded and inside there were hard uncomfortable pews and dull lighting. Our commitment was to change the environment to express the light and life of God's good news.

A church grows by attracting visitors. That's how everyone begins attending, even if they have come from another church. The only exception is for those who have grown up in that particular church. Therefore attracting and looking after visitors is of primary importance. The ten practical goals of the Fanfare Project were all aimed at making visitors welcome.

5.5 Make visitors welcome

The first of Fanfare's ten practical goals is 'We will make you welcome.' Both buildings and people need to express a welcoming atmosphere, and a climate of acceptance. Rick Warren says, 'Long before the pastor preaches, the visitors are already deciding whether or not they will come back. They are asking themselves, "Do I feel welcome here?"'[3]

Every one of the 400 people who joined our church over ten years started as a visitor. We have made a commitment to attract visitors, particularly unchurched visitors, and try to do this in a number of ways.

Instead of elders, deacons and pastors meeting for prayer up to the time of the start of worship, we pray together earlier so that there is a freedom to mix with the congregation before each service and personally welcome people. Many significant conversations take place. One of the best ways to create a positive environment and build up a sense of expectation is to greet people personally and speak to as many as you can *before* the worship service begins.

---

[3] Warren, *The Purpose-Driven Church*, p. 211.

Place some church leaders at all the entrances. Create a welcoming information point. Carefully choose those who
welcome visitors. If a church wants to attract young couples,
try to use young couples as welcomers. In larger churches, it is
possible to use a variety of age groups as welcomers. One
church uses children to welcome children.

We no longer identify visitors publicly. Established
Christians from other churches may like to be noticed, but generally speaking unchurched people don't. For some of them, it
is their worst nightmare. Welcome visitors in a general way in
the early part of the worship, and then encourage regular
members of the congregation to welcome one another. That
way, visitors feel equal with everybody else as well as being personally welcomed without the embarrassment of being publicly
recognized.

Like many churches we encourage visitors to fill in a welcome
card. We also encourage every member of the congregation to
use a simple communication card to send a message to any of
the pastors, to make prayer requests, or to provide feedback
relating to the worship.

Every visitor completing a welcome card receives a personal
letter from one of the pastors during the next week. If a visitor
is new to the neighbourhood, or is a resident who has not been
to church before, we invite them to a Newcomers Tea one
Sunday afternoon. That can be the beginning of the journey
into the church family. At that time we give them a further invitation to a Newcomers house group which meets for eight
Wednesday evenings. In a larger church, such a group provides
an opportunity for newcomers to make new friends, meet
church leaders and hear about how the church functions.

As well as creating a positive physical environment, create an
environment of acceptance and love in a practical way that visitors can actually feel. Like Jesus we can accept people without
necessarily approving of their lifestyles. We can love as Jesus
loved. Larger churches do not have to be impersonal, and it is

not true that smaller churches are always warm and welcoming. From an unchurched visitor's perspective, a smaller church may in fact be more threatening to enter than a larger church.

Rick Warren writes:

> Of course, every congregation thinks their church is loving. That's because the people who think it is unloving aren't there! Ask typical members, and they will say, 'Our church is very friendly and loving.' What they usually mean is, 'We love each other. We are friendly and loving to the people already here.' They love the people they feel comfortable with, but that warm fellowship doesn't automatically translate into love for unbelievers and visitors. Some churches point to their lack of a crowd as proof that they are biblical, orthodox, or Spirit-filled. They maintain that their small size is proof that they are a pure church, that they haven't compromised their beliefs. It may actually mean they don't love lost people enough to reach out to them. The honest reason many churches do not have a crowd is because they don't want one.[4]

5.6 Create ministries to meet needs

As mentioned earlier, Chuck Swindoll has written bluntly, 'Others will not care how much we know until they know how much we care.' Ministry needs to be a positive expression of the gospel, caring for both the congregation and the community. The New Testament asks for a church where the spiritual, physical, emotional, intellectual and social needs of people are met. It asks for a church where the members care for one another, support and encourage one another and have a strong sense of belonging.

In an increasingly fragmented society that emphasizes individualism, it is important for believers to build relationships with each other and with the community in which the church is

---

[4] Warren, *The Purpose-Driven Church*, p. 209.

placed. This not only creates a sense of community but also helps to meet the needs of both the congregation and the local people.

Most churches struggle with this. All kinds of pastoral and visitation schemes have been tried, but it seems there are always people in every church who feel overlooked, and complain they are not 'missed' when they are 'missing'. One north of England church with between 150 and 200 members wrote in a letter to me:

> There appear to be new faces in the congregation most services and we are struggling to find effective and meaningful pastoral care for them all (we have a Pastoral Friends scheme but this needs updating almost weekly).

In many churches it is expected that the minister, or the staff, the elders or the deacons, or members of the PCC (Parochial Church Council) will provide pastoral care. In a smaller church it may be possible for the minister to meet this expectation. He or she may be able to visit the hospital every day. He or she may be able to know everyone by name and be involved in their lives, to perform all the weddings and officiate at every funeral, to be present at every church committee meeting and almost every church activity. But what happens when the church grows? Two hundred members is considered to be the maximum number that one minister can truly care for. When a church reaches this size, it faces a choice. Either the members limit the size of the church to both the leadership style and the congregation's expectations of the minister, or the members learn to care for one another and exercise ministry.

As the Crystal Cathedral in California grew, Robert Schuller delegated to an associate the responsibility for training an elite group of 700 'lay ministers of pastoral care'. They were trained and officially commissioned as ministers by the congregation. Each of them was assigned to 10 to 15 families of the church for whom they were responsible.

The church in Acts was a church in which people cared for one another. 'All the believers were together and had everything in common' (Acts 2:44). 'Selling their possessions and goods, they gave to anyone as he had need' (Acts 2:45). The apostle Paul reminds believers: 'in Christ we who are many form one body, and each member belongs to all the others' (Romans 12:5).

Support groups for people coping with specific problems and hurts exercise an important caring ministry. People need to see that belonging to a church can make a real difference in how they cope. Make it a policy to set up support groups for bereavement, depression, foster parents, carers, the unemployed, single parents, and those battling with alcohol or drug addiction. Provide a team of people to carry out practical work such as mowing a lawn, cutting a hedge, cleaning a room, fetching shopping, preparing a meal, and helping with other practical tasks that elderly or ill people may not be able to do for themselves. At Frinton we are part of a community-care ministry that provides cars and drivers to transport elderly or seriously ill people to hospital or doctor's appointments. In addition a drop-in centre is available every morning of the week, providing refreshments and someone to talk to. A coffee shop is open two mornings a week. Such ministries are a positive expression of the gospel, and part of a local church's commitment to preach a positive message to a hurting community.

Pastoral care reaching beyond the church is a means of bringing people to faith in Christ. In this sense, churches need to learn to do ministry.

It is clear that breakout churches (and growing churches generally) tend to have a greater presence in their community. They are less inward looking and see the role of the church as helping people, whether they are members of their congregation or not. As a result, persons in the community are aware that the church exists and that it is available in time of need. The goals of providing ministry to the community were not designed to produce growth in these churches, but it would appear that growth can be an unintended consequence. The ministering church is seen as an open, accepting congregation, rather than a restricted social club. Further, those who have received help or support and those on the outside who have worked on joint ministry projects with the church may establish relationships with the pastor or members, come to know Christ (if they do not already), and eventually join the fellowship.[5]

---

[5] C. Kirk Hadaway, *Church Growth Principles: Separating Fact from Fiction*, Broadman 1991, p. 169.

6

Let Worship Attract the Unchurched

6.1 Design worship that is inspiring and relevant

One of the eight quality characteristics for a healthy church mentioned by Christian Schwarz in *Natural Church Development* is 'inspiring worship'.

> While the question whether a church service targets primarily non-Christians has no apparent relationship to church growth, there is indeed a strong correlation between an 'inspired worship experience' and a church's quality and quantity.[1]

Schwarz defines 'inspiring'

> to be understood in the literal sense of inspiratio and means an inspiredness which comes from the Spirit of God. Whenever the Holy Spirit is truly at work (and His presence is not merely presumed), He will have a concrete effect upon the way a worship service is conducted, including the atmosphere of a gathering. People attending truly 'inspired' services typically indicate that 'going to church is fun'.[2]

---

[1] Christian Schwarz, *Natural Church Development*, Church Smart Resources 1996, p. 31.
[2] *Ibid.*

In contrast, for many people, 'church' means dull, boring and irrelevant. Recently someone gave me a book called *101 Things to Do with a Dull Church*.[3] It's a great book and fun to read. But what that kind of book is saying is that the church has a reputation for irrelevance and boredom.

How can we change this? James White, in *Opening the Front Door: Worship and Church Growth*, 'has identified five elements of atmosphere in growing churches: celebrative, friendly, relaxed, positive, and expectant'.[4]

When an aircraft gains height after take-off, it comes to a stage in the climb where it encounters turbulence. Worship is often a point of turbulence as a church begins to reach the unchurched. It can be a painful time for both congregation and leaders. There are so many different styles and patterns of worship. Each church probably has a range of worship that fits within certain boundaries. On a scale of 1 to 100, with 1 representing informal lively charismatic worship, and 100 representing very formal, highly liturgical worship, each church probably finds itself, say, between the scale of 20 to 40, 60 to 80, 10 to 30, or 50 to 70. Few, if any, churches will embrace the full range of worship styles. The boundaries are normally set by the majority of the congregation with a few people at either end pushing in the direction they believe the church should move. Some want much more formal, traditional and quieter worship, while others want more informal, livelier, contemporary worship. These are the points of tension. A church may either extend its boundaries in both directions and embrace flexible styles of worship, or it may move both boundaries simultaneously up or down the scale.

---

[3] Martin Wroe and Adrian Reith, *101 Things to Do with a Dull Church*, IVP 1994.

[4] James White, *Opening the Front Door: Worship and Church Growth*, as quoted by Thom S. Rainer in *The Book of Church Growth*, Broadman 1993, p. 228.

Worship styles are determined by a variety of factors such as denominational affiliation, tradition, age of church, and age of congregation. Whichever style or pattern of worship a church incorporates, what is offered needs to follow the requirements given by Jesus: 'God is spirit, and his worshippers must worship in spirit and in truth' (John 4:24). I have always valued Archbishop William Temple's well-known definition of worship:

> The submission of all our nature to God; the quickening of the conscience by his holiness; the nourishment of the mind with his truth; the purifying of the imagination by his beauty; the opening of the heart to his love; the surrender of the will to his purpose.[5]

Broadly speaking, there are several church categories:

- Traditional.
- Contemporary.
- Blended: a mix of traditional and contemporary.
- Seeker-sensitive.
- Seeker-centred.
- Multiple-track: offering more than one style of worship.

As there is no one correct style, many churches incorporate elements of more than one format. It is a mistake to think that only one type of church can be effective during the twenty-first century.

Traditional churches with a commitment to excellence and relevance can have a strong appeal to many people. They can at the same time incorporate a seeker-sensitive element.

Contemporary churches are often those which encourage congregational participation, and use mainly modern music and songs. They are not necessarily seeker-sensitive. They do have a strong emphasis on all-age worship.

---

[5] William Temple, *Preachings in St. John's Gospel*, Macmillan 1939, p. 68.

Blended churches incorporate elements of both traditional and contemporary churches and frequently meet the needs of both old and young. These churches often give people time to accept change. Blended churches often end up with a more contemporary style of worship, but by initially blending styles, provide people with an opportunity to adjust.

Seeker-sensitive churches focus on relevance. They are not the same as seeker-centred churches which concentrate almost exclusively on reaching the unchurched. Seeker-sensitive churches tend to have a simple structure which is flexible and creative. They focus on inspirational preaching and applying biblical teaching to the everyday needs of people. They can be either traditional or contemporary.

Seeker-centred churches emphasize evangelism. They are more on the pioneering front than the seeker-sensitive churches and have little or no congregational participation. Instead they focus on presentation from the front rather than worship offered by the congregation. These churches often have a clear sense of purpose, an evangelistic agenda set by the unchurched, casual informal worship with relevant teaching and contemporary music.

Multiple-track churches may offer three or four worship services of different styles, each targeted to reach a specific group of people. One pastor described his multiple-track services as traditional, loud, louder and loudest!

Whatever your preferred style, the prophet's experience in Isaiah 6:1–8 describes a pattern of worship that is worth following. It starts with Isaiah having an overwhelming sense of the presence of God. Every worship service needs to start with a clear reminder that we are in God's presence. The call to worship and the first songs can bring God's presence to mind. Having become aware of who God is, Isaiah then becomes aware of who he is, 'a man of unclean lips'. Praise and adoration is therefore followed by confession. The confession is from the heart and is followed by the assurance of God's cleansing and forgiveness: 'your guilt is taken away and your sin atoned for'. Next comes the word: 'Then I heard the voice of the Lord saying "Whom shall I send? And who will go for us?"' Finally the response of obedience: 'Here am I. Send me!' It would be wonderful if every member of the congregation was so inspired to action!

One of the weakest elements in many worship services is linking together the various sections of the worship. This detracts from the purpose of designing worship for the Holy Spirit to inspire. Give careful attention to linking together the various items of a worship service. I agree with Rick Warren when he says:

> Almost all churches need to pick up the pace of their services. Television has permanently shortened the attention span. . . . most churches move at a snail's pace. There is a lot of 'dead time' between different elements. Work on minimising transitional times. As soon as one element ends, another should begin.[6]

This is important in gaining the confidence of the unchurched, and also focuses believers on what they are there for. Untidy, unprepared worship does not glorify God. Prayerfully and carefully prepared worship enables the Holy Spirit to work through the leaders who have prepared for the service, and it does not rule out spontaneity.

I have become aware through my involvement in televised worship of how much time can be wasted. At Frinton there have been a number of occasions when we have broadcast our worship services live on national television and radio. On all of these occasions we have surprised ourselves at how many elements of worship can be included in under an hour. On Easter Sunday 1997 we broadcast our second service on the UK ITV network. The worship included eight hymns and songs, the

---

[6] Rick Warren, *The Purpose-Driven Church*, Zondervan 1995, p. 255.

baptism by immersion of four people, each of whom told their story and were prayed for individually, a children's message, a children's song, a sung duet, three prayer times, a twelve-minute sermon and a closing prayer. All within 55 minutes and 40 seconds! That is not to say that worship services should be less than one hour, but it does illustrate how much time is usually wasted. More interestingly, and perhaps more significantly, the response of both the congregation in church and the viewers and listeners at home, has been that the worship did not seem hurried. The many letters and telephone calls we received following our occasions 'on air' have taught us that commitment to excellence is a commitment that God can use powerfully.

If the church is to be healthy it must offer a quality of worship that fortifies the values of the believer and at the same time attracts, appeals, and relates to the unchurched. From the first days of the Christian church, both unbelievers and believers have been present in worship: 'So if the whole church comes together . . . or some unbelievers come in . . .' (1 Corinthians 14:23).

Worship services have become the biggest barrier to the unchurched. This includes the whole worship experience, the physical environment, poor music, whether produced by an organ or a music group, as well as irrelevant sermons. It can all be a turn-off to the unchurched. Boring, predictable and lifeless worship, along with sermons which are irrelevant to every day are some of the reasons why many have either left the church or show little or no interest in attending.

Rick Warren says, 'Making a service comfortable for the unchurched doesn't mean changing your theology. It means changing the environment.'[7] The biblical principle is clear. Although worship is an activity of believers, it can be a constructive and relevant witness to unbelievers. How can we make

---

[7] *Ibid.*, p. 244.

sure this is the case? It will not necessarily be by changing the style of worship. The experience of many churches is that the quality, not the style, of worship makes it worthwhile for both believer and unbeliever. Whether the style is traditional, contemporary or charismatic, a commitment to excellence changes worship from a negative to a positive experience.

The start of the service is important: 'if the trumpet does not sound a clear call, who will get ready for battle?' (1 Corinthians 14:8). Paul continues: 'Unless you speak intelligible words with your tongue, how will anyone know what you are saying? You will just be speaking into the air.'

Have a clear, confident beginning to a positive worship experience. Too many church services start like a damp squib. The leader ambles into the service. Sometimes the leaders' voices are not clear, either because they have misjudged the strength of their voice, or the sound system has not been tested before the service. Some services begin with a catalogue of notices. If the worship service is to be a witness, let it express confidence, energy, enthusiasm and expectancy. Believers may be tolerant of poor-quality worship, but unbelievers often expect more.

Answers to a number of questions should guide what happens in a worship service:

1. What traditions of worship should be maintained, and why?
2. What variations (interviews, changes in the order of service, video clips, people telling their stories) will be included?
3. What's in it for the single mother, the teenager, the unemployed, the first-time visitor?
4. What significant items can fill otherwise dead spots when people are approaching or leaving the platform?
5. What congregational participation is appropriate in addition to singing and taking offerings?
6. How should we improve the 'blips' that occurred in the

previous week's service (e.g. interminably long prayers, the public address system not working properly)?

7. How can we streamline some tedious moments (such as extended remarks when introducing items of worship, too many announcements and weather remarks)?

8. What notice should we take of the Christian calendar?

9. How should we provide for the varying musical tastes so that we achieve balance and quality?

7

Lead the Church to Enlarge its Vision

7.1 Build a positive leadership team

When the aircraft was climbing away from the runway, encountering some turbulence, its nose up, getting ready to make a 90-degree turn, my instructor would say firmly to me, 'Don't be frightened of the aircraft. Handle it in a confident and positive way. Make the aircraft do what you want it to do.'

Now that's not a good model for leadership, yet there are similarities. Some leaders are frightened to take the lead. The role of the leadership in shaping the spiritual climate of the church is vital, and is not something from which we can abdicate. Serving the church through leadership is about clearly defining, communicating and applying the purposes of the church to the membership. It's about building people up, inspiring them, motivating them, encouraging them, and 'preparing God's people for works of service' (Ephesians 4:12).

> Leadership is influence. It's not position. It's not title. It's the ability to influence people so they will follow. If somebody is following me, I'm a leader. If they're not following me, I'm not a leader.[1]

---

[1] John Maxwell, *Growing Churches*, Autumn 1995, p. 5.

There are books written entirely about leadership, and therefore my concern here is simply to underline the importance of positive leadership in building a healthy church.

The task of church leadership is to discover and remove growth-restricting diseases and barriers so that natural, normal growth can occur. Seventy years ago Roland Allen, in his classic text on missions, called this kind of growth 'the spontaneous expansion of the church.' It is the kind of growth reported in the book of Acts.[2]

The first 'quality characteristic' listed by Christian Schwarz in his list of eight quality characteristics is 'empowering leadership'. 'Leaders of growing churches concentrate on empowering other Christians for ministry.'[3] In other words, do not use church members to help you achieve your own purposes and goals. Instead equip members to identify their ministries and the spiritual potential God has given them.

Leadership can be painful. You can get hurt. It can be frustrating, humbling and lonely. However, the responsibility for the health of a church ultimately falls on the leadership. Peter Wagner's book *Leading Your Church to Growth* states: 'The primary catalytic factor for growth in a local church is the pastor.' Wagner further says that strong pastoral leadership is the first of many church growth signs of health: 'Vital Sign Number One of a healthy church is a pastor who is a possibility thinker and whose dynamic leadership has been used to catalyse the entire church into action for growth.'[4]

7.2 Provide a vision for the church

This often means changing both the role of the minister, and the congregation's perception of what the minister should be

---

[2] Rick Warren, *The Purpose-Driven Church*, Zondervan 1995, p. 17.
[3] Christian Schwarz, *Natural Church Development*, Church Smart Resources 1996, p. 22.
[4] C. Peter Wagner, *Leading Your Church to Growth*, Regal 1984.

doing. What is expected of ministers was a key issue at a 24-hour consultation of ministers of larger churches in the summer of 1997. Nearly everyone present expressed some sense of frustration, and admitted to feelings of failure and guilt, while at the same time realizing they had a key role to play if the church was to grow. This was because church members' traditional expectations of the clergy are so numerous that most ministers live with a permanent sense of guilt. Most I have spoken to over the years are driven by deadlines, overwhelmed by numerous committees and a calendar of events that created both a sense of failure, and also the frustration of being unable to focus on the big picture of what church is all about.

Preaching plays an important role in providing a vision. Though preaching need not be done only by the senior minister, growing churches are often motivated by a minister who takes the lion's share of this responsibility. There may be equally well qualified and more effective preachers besides the senior minister, but if the preaching role is divided less than 50:50 with others, experience demonstrates that different imprints will be left on the congregation, even though all the leaders may share the same vision for the church.

Steve Chalke writes:

The big question a preacher should ask is not 'what should I preach about this Sunday?', but 'where are we going as a church over the next 12 months, and how do we get there?' The majority of sermons should simply serve as a tool of this vision. In reality, a church with no strategic plan and direction will always be one that, in the final analysis, wastes the preaching opportunities presented to its leaders Sunday by Sunday. It's only when a church's leadership has carefully developed its strategy that they are in a position to determine the content of their preaching diary. Only after answering three key questions –'where are we?', 'where are we going?' and 'how are we going to get there?' – is it possible to ascertain what you should be preaching and teaching about on a regular basis.[5]

This takes time. Leith Anderson sums up exactly the dilemma that many of us feel as our church grows beyond a certain size:

> When I was the pastor of a church with 200 in attendance, I felt very important in parishioners' lives. I stopped by the community hospital every day whether anyone from the church was there or not. I checked the admission roster just in case. When babies were born in the middle of the night, fathers often called me before calling the grandparents. I knew everyone by name and I was integrally involved in many lives. I performed all church weddings and officiated at every church funeral. I was present at every church committee meeting and almost every church activity. Now, as the pastor of a church of thousands, I am not nearly so important to most people. Since it is impossible to have a hub with thousands of spokes, the large majority of parishioners are relationally connected to someone else. Other pastors do the majority of baptisms, weddings and funerals. I cannot call most people by name. I can't remember the last time I received a call in the middle of the night, announcing, 'It's a girl, and you're the first one I've called!' Now they call someone else. There are days when I grieve the loss of earlier relationships and importance, but I have chosen to continually modify my style of leadership and set of relationships to fit the needs and growth of the church.[6]

What are the alternatives as a church begins to grow? You can limit the size of the church to the leadership style and relationship needs of the clergy. You could change the minister so that the church can find someone who relates differently, while

---

[5] Steve Chalke, *Alpha* magazine, July 1996, p. 23.
[6] Leith Anderson, *A Church for the Twenty-First Century*, Bethany House 1992, p. 177.

the outgoing minister finds another church to fit his or her style. Or you can push a minister to be personally responsible for more and more people until he or she burns out. Since most clergy and churches choose the first option, the majority of our churches stay small in number. Even if they grow larger, they often plateau at the 250 to 300 level. The problem is you cannot run a larger church as though it were a smaller church. Some ministers who try to manage a congregation of 500 or more as if it were a church of 100 or 200 find themselves working very long hours with enormous commitment, and possible eventual exhaustion.

Most researchers and writers on church growth view the clergy as having a key role. George Barna in *User Friendly Churches* says:

> User friendly churches invariably had a strong pastor leading the church. 'Strong' means that the pastor was in control and was a true leader. 'Pastor' refers to one who understood the needs of the congregation and the target audience and provided the necessary vision and spiritual guidance. A strong pastor is one who takes charge of the church without breaking the spirit of those who wish to be involved.[7]

Such leaders are role models. Here are three examples of that kind of leadership. Robert Schuller has influenced many, in spite of the criticism he receives for his expansive and expensive Crystal Cathedral and the preaching style and content of his weekly televised service. To give him credit, Schuller arrived in California in 1955, with just $500, to test certain church-growth principles he believed were valid. By 1984 the church already had 10,000 members.

Robert Schuller significantly influenced Bill Hybels of Willow Creek Community Church in southern Chicago. In

---

[7] George Barna, *User Friendly Churches*, Regal 1991, p. 143.

their book *Rediscovering Church* Lynne and Bill Hybels tell the
story of Willow Creek. At one point, under the heading of
'Divine Encounter', Lynne tells how in 1976, Bill took his staff
and lay leaders to Schuller's church in Garden Grove, southern
California, for a pastors' conference:

> During the conference, our entire entourage somehow ended up in
> Robert Schuller's office, which at that time was in the upper floors
> of the Tower of Prayer. Bill told Dr. Schuller about our efforts to
> establish a church for the unchurched and about our seeker ser-
> vices and about our tentative plans to buy land for a future build-
> ing. Bill asked Dr. Schuller if he could give us any advice
> regarding our next step. Dr. Schuller answered, 'If you give God
> a thimble, perhaps He will choose it. If you give God a five-gallon
> bucket, perhaps He will choose to fill that. If you give Him a fifty-
> gallon drum, perhaps He will choose to do something extraordi-
> nary and fill even that. If God chooses to do a miracle, you'd
> better be ready for it. Don't buy a thimbleful of land. Buy a fifty-
> gallon drum.'

Lynne continues:

> Was there any logic in that counsel? By all rights it was ridiculous
> for a ragtag bunch of kids like us to dream even of a thimble. And
> here we were, huddled in that sky-high office, committing ourselves
> to the pursuit of a fifty-gallon drum. Had we been mesmerised by
> the emotional appeal of a clever communicator? Had we been lured
> into a dream that was more about self-aggrandisement than obedi-
> ence to God? Had we been 'puffed up' with the affirmation offered
> us by a man so highly esteemed – the only credible adult who had
> given us any encouragement? Had we become victims of our own
> youthful enthusiasm? ... As I look back through the years I can't
> help but think that what happened that day was exactly what we
> thought it was at the time: a divinely staged encounter. We returned
> home changed. We had been given a glimpse of the future, an aug-
> mented sense of destiny, and it catapulted us forward. We were
> humbled by the responsibilities and potential challenges, yet we

were excited by the possibilities and convinced anew of our unmis-
takable calling.[8]

The third example is Rick Warren who was also influenced
by Schuller at the beginning of the Saddleback Church.

I began Saddleback by going door-to-door for twelve weeks and
surveying the unchurched in my area. Six years earlier I had read
Robert Schuller's book 'Your Church Has Real Possibilities',
which told how he had gone door-to-door in 1955 and asked hundreds of people, 'Why don't you go to church?' and 'What do you
want in a church?' I thought this was a great idea but felt the questions needed to be rephrased for the more skeptical 1980s. I wrote
down in my notebook five questions I would use to start
Saddleback.[9]

These three examples of leadership show, as many others in
larger churches, that a strong sense of commitment to one
church over a long period of time, and a strong sense of God's
call, helps towards building a strong church.

The Kingsway International Christian Centre in Hackney,
east London, meets in a converted warehouse. It is the largest
church building to be opened in Britain for a hundred years.
Since it began in 1993 the congregation has swelled from 300 to
a staggering 5,000. The pastor, Nigerian-born Matthew
Ashomolowo, arrived in the UK in 1984. When he started he
had just eleven people in the congregation. Now there are six
other satellite churches, and plans for further expansion.

Dr Larry Michael, a former associate pastor with me at
Tonbridge Baptist Church, now the senior pastor of a growing
church in the USA and a lecturer at Beeson Divinity School,
Samford University, says that theology is the foundation of

---

[8] Lynne and Bill Hybels, *Rediscovering Church*, Zondervan 1995, p. 69.
[9] Warren, *The Purpose-Driven Church*, p. 190.

church growth, and leadership is the catalyst of church growth. Leaders must be spiritual in orientation, skilled in implementation, and positive in motivation.

7.3 Stay spiritually focused

Leadership in healthy, growing churches requires deep spiritual commitment. The first priority of leadership is a close personal relationship with God. Leaders must protect their own spiritual journey with God which is the foundation of their leadership. When the Sanhedrin questioned the apostles, and 'saw the courage of Peter and John and realised that they were unschooled, ordinary men, they were astonished and they took note that these men had been with Jesus' (Acts 4:13). Many rapidly growing churches have a leadership who give large amounts of time to prayer, despite their busy schedules.

Leaders can help others by sharing something of their own spiritual journey, by being actively involved in pastoral ministry and personal evangelism, and by setting an example in giving. Their integrity is essential: behaviour, character, credibility, conviction, attitude and self-control are all important. Personal qualities for leadership are spelled out in the New Testament in such passages as 1 Timothy 3.

Leaders need to avoid theological and emotional extremes. They need balance in their use of time, between administration and the care of people, between family and work commitments. None of this is easy; it is a matter of discipline and self-control.

7.4 Develop skills of implementation

As well as being a communicator, the leader seeks to be an equipper. The need to involve and mobilize all church members in ministry and to nurture other leaders is vital; how to do this is the subject of a later chapter.

In 1977 Lyle Schaller described pastors as ranchers. 'In a church led by a rancher the sheep are still shepherded, but the rancher does not do it. The rancher sees that it is done by others.'[10]

Leaders should aim to equip rather than enable. 'An enabler is a relatively uninvolved technician who understands the process by which things are accomplished and who enables others to achieve goals.'[11]

> An equipper actively sets goals for a congregation according to the will of God, obtains goal ownership from the people, and sees that each church member is properly motivated and equipped to do his or her part in accomplishing the goals.[12]

You can only do this if you are willing to share ministry. One of the hindrances to growth in some churches is the leadership's, or clergy's, unwillingness to let go of ministry. One of the most exciting principles of church health is releasing others to do the work of ministry.

It becomes easier if you know your own gifts, abilities and limitations. Develop your skills and show to others what you want to teach them. Practise ministry, model it, but be willing to involve others in it. Too much time spent in the study and it becomes a dangerous place from which to lead the church. That is because you need to know your people. Put people first and develop relationships of trust. Be available and approachable. Find ways of helping yourself to remember names. Pray for church members by name on a regular basis. Use cards and photographs to help you memorize who is who.

Finally, spend time planning. This is one of the biggest

---

[10] Warren, *The Purpose-Driven Church*, p. 59.
[11] Richard G. Hutcheson Jr, *The Wheel Within the Wheel: Confronting the Management Crisis of the Pluralist Church*, p. 54.
[12] Wagner, *Leading Your Church to Growth*, p. 79.

challenges in building a healthy church. But if the leader doesn't know where he or she is going, neither will the church family. Don't be afraid of setting goals. We set financial goals, so we can set people goals in line with the purposes of the church. I have discovered that the more our church grows, the more I have to review my priorities and realize that people and planning are top of the agenda. Relating to people and steering the church, under the guidance of the Holy Spirit, are of paramount importance. As healthy churches grow, senior ministers will find the need to make adjustments constantly, protecting their time with God, with people, and with planning.

> Nothing discourages a church more than not knowing why it exists. On the other hand, the quickest way to reinvigorate a plateaued or declining church is to reclaim God's purpose for it and help the members understand the great tasks the church has been given by Christ.[13]

If a church is to be healthy and experience growth, then the leader needs the time and skills to focus on major planning, policy-making, appointment and care of other leaders, the financial objectives of the church, and the decisions that shape the future of the church's mission and outreach.

In the past, ministers have sometimes been too busy to give time to these matters; they have not been trained in the necessary skills, and may have left these things totally to lay leaders whose business skills may seem better than the minister's. Clergy certainly need the insights, experience and skills of fellow-leaders, but they cannot abdicate these responsibilities if the church is to grow. The evidence is that healthy growing churches have senior staff who are very much involved in planning and policy-making.

---

[13] Warren, *The Purpose-Driven Church*, p. 87.

7.5 Be positive in motivation

Visionary leaders become positive about the future, because they believe God has given a vision of that future. I have discovered that people respond to vision more than to need.

Good leaders not only have vision and a sense of purpose, but they are also able to recruit, train and equip others to implement the vision. Effective leaders have the ability to see the vision clearly; to say it continuously; and to show it creatively. Vision and purpose inspire people. They bring people together. So you need to understand God's purpose for your church.

As with preaching, have a passionate enthusiasm. Leaders must have initiative and be self-starters. They need to be proactive and not reactive. If the leadership is not positive, it is unlikely that the congregation will be. Negative leaders attract negative thinking members to their congregations, and negative congregations resist change. The role of leaders to be positive about the Christian message and the potential of the church is essential. Of course there are times when members of the clergy feel depressed, but if that cannot be overcome, or if that attitude is permanently present, the question must be asked: 'Is this kind of leadership consistent with the leadership attitudes of the New Testament?'

To inspire and motive other leaders and to inspire a waiting congregation to worship God with energy and hope requires a positive attitude. It is irresponsible to subject the congregation to our own particular moods. That does not mean we have to be false. It does mean we need to ask God, as David did in Psalm 51: 'restore to me the joy of your salvation.'

7.6 Have a servant heart

At the same time, however, leaders need an unreserved submission to the lordship of Christ. 'Paradoxically, the Christian leader must be the ultimate follower, a follower of the Leader himself.'[14] Following Christ is following the greatest follower of all. It is summed up in those well-known phrases found in Philippians 2:6–8:

> Who, being in very nature God, did not consider equality with God something to be grasped, but made himself nothing, taking the very nature of a servant, being made in human likeness. And being found in appearance as a man, he humbled himself and became obedient to death – even death on a cross!

Jesus invited Peter, Andrew, James and John not to become leaders but followers. This quality for leadership demonstrates a servant heart, a willingness to learn, to admit when wrong, to listen, and above all to view leadership as servanthood. Strong leadership is not dictatorship. Strong leadership is having a teachable spirit and a willingness to be accountable.

Accountability means encouraging others to ask tough questions. Leaders, as well as being followers, need other followers to support them. Leith Anderson says:

> Moses was one of God's most magnificent leaders, but he never would have made it without the support of faithful followers. The best of followers ask the hardest questions. They ask their leaders whether they are spending adequate time in prayer, whether they are filled with the Holy Spirit, whether they are resisting sexual temptation, whether they are faithful to the Bible, whether they are correctly handling their money, whether they are getting enough rest and exercise, and whether they are growing intellectually. Such questions are direct and personal. Thus, how they are asked makes a great deal of difference. Followers must first earn the right to ask accountability questions.[15]

---

[14] William D. Lawrence, *Growing Churches*, No. 14, Summer 1995.
[15] Anderson, *A Church for the Twenty-First Century*, p. 231.

Effective leaders will be teachable, accountable, and will accept responsibility for themselves and for those under their care. Above all, they will make prayer a priority.

7.7 Lead for growth and not control

The task of a leader is to lead the church, not to control it. When the leadership controls then the leaders become a bottleneck hindering growth. Every church must decide whether it is going to be structured for control or for growth. In some churches it will be painful for elders, deacons, parish councils and clergy to face up to this question. Most churches I know have been structured for control. Elders and deacons and parish councils end up as policing bodies.

Leadership is about setting people free for ministry. It also means actually doing ministry and not just discussing it or making decisions about others involved in it. For a church to grow the leadership must give up control of the ministry, and the people must give up control of the leadership. Rick Warren says he still has 67 founding members of the Saddleback Church in membership. These are members whom he used to visit regularly. He would have meals in their homes, invite them to his home, socialize with them. Now they may not shake hands with him more than once a year. But, he says, they have given up that control as they believe God's church and its task of reaching the lost is more important. It takes unselfish people to enable the church to grow. Learn how to give up control. We discovered at Frinton that when we grew to over 500 members, no one person, minister, elder or deacon could know everything that was going on.

At Frinton Free Church we agreed that our elders meetings in particular would be shaped more for prayer and ministry than discussion and minor decision-making. Until then, we had often found our monthly leadership meeting was taken up with the pastoral concerns about individual church members, which in one sense was helpful, but limited if all we did was talk about them. We appointed a team of nine pastoral assistants under the leadership of one elder. Only those pastoral matters that affected the whole church were then brought to this monthly leaders meeting. The elders, in turn, trusted the pastoral assistants to do pastoral ministry. This, along with the discipline of not discussing other details of church life, left the leaders free to discuss major policy issues, the direction and strategies of the church as a whole, and to be creative thinkers and prayers. Each month we made a point of placing a major new initiative at the top of the agenda.

Ministers, elders and deacons also needed to be seen to be involved in the actual ministry of the church. For too long they had been viewed simply as a discussion-based policing body, rather than as leaders involved in ministry. At Frinton we felt a particular responsibility to lead the congregation in the building of relationships, both within the church and the community. We needed to model patterns of ministry that others could learn from. On Sundays we created space to pray early before each service so that there was time to meet members of the congregation as they arrived. Many significant conversations take place prior to the commencement of worship that benefit both people and leaders.

PART
2

*Equip People
for Effective Ministry*

8

Get the Church on Course

8.1 Help believers to build a strong relationship with God

When an aircraft is flying the airfield circuit it reaches a point in the climb when it makes a 90-degree turn. It then continues to climb to the circuit height, or altitude. Whether the aircraft is flying the circuit or taking a longer journey, this continued climb towards a cruising altitude is taking the aircraft towards the desired level flightpath. Likewise, leading believers towards spiritual maturity is getting the church on course.

The key issue is not church growth, but church health. As the church is a 'body', it is alive and therefore, like most living things, it grows naturally. Our task therefore is to care for its health in the same way that a parent cares for the health of a child, providing nourishment and removing hindrances to natural growth. When churches are healthy, they grow in the way God wants them to grow.

How do we help people to build a strong relationship with God? Whenever I look out over our congregation I think of all the potential it has. A minister can easily assume that the majority of the membership are not interested in building a strong relationship with God; or, particularly in a larger church, that many people are not interested in anything beyond

105

attending worship. However, realistically more people are keen to develop their faith but don't know how, or they haven't realized their own potential in Christ. God desires that each believer should grow in knowledge and experience, so a pastor's prime responsibility is to lead people towards spiritual maturity. Many pastors therefore wish they had more time to spend with individual church members. New pastors just out of theological college often find themselves caught up in so many pastoral duties and preaching commitments that they ask the question 'Just how do I go about building these people up in their relationship with God?'

Sermons and Bible studies don't seem to achieve the goal. Christians who have heard thousands of sermons and have an outstanding knowledge of the Bible sometimes appear to be indifferent to involvement in the church, have a judgemental attitude, or when the pressure is on, collapse like a pack of cards. Some of these people know their Bibles from cover to cover and hardly ever miss a worship service. So what's the problem?

As Christian Schwarz reminds us: 'pure doctrine alone, as countless examples illustrate, does not induce growth'.[1] In other words, knowledge alone is not enough. Spiritual growth is not automatic. Although in one sense I had always known this, I was in ministry many years before this truth really dawned on me and I consciously faced up to it. When I shared this with other leaders in our church, I could see that although like me they had always known it, the reality had not registered with them either, and they were excited about what we might do about it. I am convinced that many churches have acted either as though spiritual growth is automatic or that their members simply do not want to grow. Apart from Bible study groups

---

[1] Christian Schwarz, *Natural Church Development*, Church Smart Resources 1996, p. 27.

churches make little or no provision to help members grow towards maturity.

Another mistake is to believe that maturity occurs instantly. A follow-up course after conversion, or an introduction to the Holy Spirit by the laying on of hands, is a powerful, meaningful and necessary ministry, but the Bible clearly teaches that spiritual growth is a longer process. Many apparently Spirit-filled believers act in ways that are contrary to the attitudes, character and spirit of Jesus. If growth were automatic and instant, why does the Bible spend so much time teaching the *process* of growth? In today's instant society the temptation for many believers is to look for short cuts to spiritual maturity. God takes time over our growth because he has such big plans for us. He allows events and circumstances into our lives to enable us to grow. These events can often be unwelcome, but God's intention is that we should grow through coping with the circumstances. We may look back and marvel at how we coped; we are stronger than we were before the event. God takes us along step by step.

Spiritual development is often a painful process. Therefore, churches need to develop strategies for helping people to grow. Christians grow best where there is ground to grow on. Our task is to help them to understand that their relationship with God is a lifelong journey. At Frinton we begin as soon as anyone starts to attend worship, by inviting them to attend a Newcomers house group which meets each Wednesday evening for approximately eight weeks. These groups are held three times a year, and provide newcomers with a 'way in' to the church.

In a larger church this 'way in' becomes vitally important, otherwise newcomers are left to fend for themselves. If they are mature believers coming from a church in another town, they may feel comfortable to find their own 'way in'. But not necessarily so, and if they are unchurched visitors, they definitely need to be helped to feel comfortable. The people are many and the place and activities may be a culture shock. Our Newcomers group meets in the senior minister's home, giving him the advantage of getting to know the people. Obviously, this in turn helps the newcomers to get to know the church leaders. Aided by a folder of notes, each group covers what we believe the Bible teaches about being a Christian and the importance of belonging to a local church family. We also talk about baptism and communion. We tell them about our particular church, its history, how the church is structured, and why we do things the way we do. We tell them about our strategy for mission, how we plan our worship and what we believe to be our purposes. We explain how belonging to a church of 500 members is a different experience to belonging to a church of 50 members. We ask them to reflect on whether our church is the church for them. Often people who have been members of churches in other parts of the country, particularly if they come from another Baptist church, assume that our church is just like the one they left. That means they could join us with a false set of expectations and they may become frustrated. We welcome the experiences and gifts new people bring into the church. Until we ran this house group we were actually losing visitors because we were not helping them to find their 'way in'.

From the Newcomers group people have a number of options. They may choose to go to an Alpha group to learn Christian basics, to attend a Baptism class if they have never been baptized, or they may be ready for church membership and choose to join a more permanent Bible study house group.

We have other small 'specialist' groups in the church to help members develop their faith and their relationship with God and with people. We are committed to small groups because we believe that this is where the strength and potential of our church lies. Christianity is relational. It is all about our relationship with God and our relationships with others. Bible knowledge is vital but by itself it is not enough. Rick Warren says, 'It takes a variety of spiritual experiences with God to produce spiritual maturity.'[2] He suggests five questions we need to ask about whatever method we choose to help people to grow:

1. Are people learning the content and meaning of the Bible?
2. Are people seeing themselves, life, and other people more clearly from God's perspective?
3. Are people's values becoming aligned with God's values?
4. Are people becoming more skilled in serving God?
5. Are people becoming more like Christ?

It is important to start something on a small scale and build on it. Don't put a huge plan into operation immediately. Let it grow. As it is never easy to develop a strategy for the spiritual growth of every member of the church, we need to learn from other successful models and adapt principles that others have found helpful.

8.2 Learn from other churches

We have learned from and applied some of the principles applied in the Saddleback Valley Community Church in southern California, one of the two largest churches in America. Rick Warren, the senior pastor, has allowed me to summarize their approach.

The Saddleback Community Church began in 1980. Three years later, they celebrated Easter with 1,000 in attendance. Now, 19 years later, they have planted over 28 new churches. For the first 15 years of its life, the Saddleback church had no permanent home. They moved 57 times into rented accommodation. In 1995 they finally moved into their own buildings. The average attendance, when I first visited in 1997, was 14,000, spread over four identical worship services. It is now 15,000 over five weekend services. What is most significant is that 80

---

[2] Rick Warren, *The Purpose-Driven Church*, Zondervan 1995, p. 340.

per cent of the large membership was previously unchurched. These are people who have been converted and baptized at Saddleback (over 6,000 in the past six years) and are not Christians transferring membership from other churches.

From the very beginning, Saddleback set out to reach the unchurched. The principles in Rick's book *The Purpose-Driven Church* have been adapted by many churches around the world, including our own. The principles are practical and biblical and adaptable into almost any culture in the world. Rick has taught these principles to over 115,000 church leaders in 42 countries and 100 denominations. He is greatly gifted and the church he leads can be a model for reaching the unchurched. If we are humble enough we can learn from this example. In 1 Thessalonians 1:6–7 Paul says: 'You became imitators of us and of the Lord. . . . And so you became a model to all the believers in Macedonia and Achaia.' Church relations are all about learning from one another and resourcing one another. Rick pleads that others do not simply copy the methods of Saddleback.

> To understand the methods, you need to understand the context in which they were developed. Otherwise you might be tempted to copy things we did without considering the context. *Please do not do this!* Instead, look beneath the methods to see the transferable principles on which they are based.[3]

Saddleback Church is built on a five-step strategy that attracts and wins the unchurched, develops them to spiritual maturity, equips them for a ministry, and then helps them establish a life mission in the world. A simple baseball diamond is used as a visual road map to help people understand their journey with God. Each base in the diamond represents a point of growth. The first base is a class on church *membership* calling for a commitment to Saddleback's membership covenant. The

---

[3] Warren, *The Purpose-Driven Church*, p. 27.

second base is a class leading to making a commitment to a *spiritual growth* covenant. Third base is a *ministry* class leading to a commitment to serve in the ministry of the church. Members then move back to the home plate by completing a class on *mission* and making a commitment to sharing their faith in the community and workplace and on mission trips. The fifth step in the overall strategy is to learn how to celebrate God's presence through *worship*.

These five steps are translated into five departments of church life:

- *Membership:* to incorporate God's family into our fellowship.
- *Maturity:* to educate God's people through discipleship.
- *Ministry:* to demonstrate God's love through service.
- *Mission:* to communicate God's word through evangelism.
- *Magnification:* to celebrate God's presence through worship.

These departments reflect the purpose of Saddleback Church: 'To bring people to Jesus and *membership* in his family, develop them to Christlike *maturity*, and equip them for their *ministry* in the church and life *mission* in the world, in order to *magnify* God's name.'

This strategy is used for helping people who are unchurched and uncommitted to become mature believers who fulfil their ministry in the church and mission in the world. The five steps of this strategy are not only reflected in the five departments of church life, but in every small group, and the five elements are encouraged in the life of each individual believer. Each believer is encouraged to know they belong, they are growing towards maturity, they are involved in a ministry, they are serving in mission, and they are magnifying God's name in worship. These are believed to be the five tasks that Christ commissioned his church to accomplish, based on Matthew 22:37–40 and 28:19–20.

Rick Warren says that growing, healthy churches have a clear-cut identity. The five purposes of Saddleback Church are clearly communicated to the congregation and the community.

8.3 Provide practical tools to help Christians grow

The strategy of the Saddleback church provides people with a sense of movement. It is attractive because most believers do not want to stand still. Even some of our most complacent church members can be frustrated by spiritual dryness. The Christian life is a journey. All too often, however, Christians do not know how to move forward on this journey and need practical help. Sadly, many clergy and church leaders do not know how to provide it. The Saddleback strategy provides a road for people to travel. The principle is both biblical and practical. Almost any sized church in any culture can adapt it and use the five steps as a model for growth.

At Frinton, our strategy for building strong believers includes a course, meeting each Wednesday evening for eight weeks, called 'Towards Christian Maturity'. It is adaptable for people at various stages of spiritual growth, and is suitable for people who have made a commitment and come to faith in Christ through an Alpha course. It has also proved to be helpful to people who have been Christians for many years. Our approach is that the road to Christian maturity is a lifelong journey. Hopefully, we are always travelling along it. Spiritual maturity is a constant theme in the apostle Paul's letters to the churches. To the church at Philippi he says concerning his own journey:

> Not that I have . . . already been made perfect, but I press on to take hold of that for which Christ Jesus took hold of me. . . . Forgetting what is behind and straining towards what is ahead, I press on towards the goal to win the prize for which God has called me heavenwards in Christ Jesus. All of us who are mature should take such a view of things. (Philippians 3:12–15)

Adapting material from various sources, including material from the Saddleback church, our 'Towards Christian Maturity' house group covers practical ways of studying and applying the Bible, building a deepening relationship with God through times of reflection, how to maintain an effective prayer life, learning how to relate to others as members of the body of Christ, and how giving is part of the believer's relationship with Christ and the church. Although these are basic elements of the Christian life, every Christian can grow in each of these areas. Older as well as newer Christians have enthusiastically attended this course. Knowing that it lasts for a specified period of eight weeks has its own attraction. It is long enough for people to bond and most groups are reluctant to end. Along with other specialist groups it is set in the context of our normal weekly house groups. Some people have opted out of their house groups for the course, and some people have been encouraged to join a regular house group having been part of this one.

Some churches find weekly house groups attract the same people year after year and the pattern is difficult to break. We have discovered that our eight-week courses do break this mould and bring together people who do not normally meet, and in the case of a larger church like ours, may not even have met before. That in itself becomes a practical help in teaching what fellowship is all about. This course, along with the Newcomers group, Alpha and other special groups runs three times a year and hundreds of church members have benefited. The practical material not only provides knowledge, or confirms knowledge people already have, but provides them with the tools to apply it. It is this 'how to do it' approach that has been welcomed. It demonstrates that what has been missing in many churches is teaching about the application of belief to the Christian life. People welcome being shown how to grow as a Christian with practical teaching about Bible study, prayer, giving and belonging to the church family.

9

Motivate Members to Serve

9.1 A strategy for every-member ministry

This is the longest part of the flight. When the aircraft has reached cruising altitude, the pilot settles down for the long haul. Now the pilot's task is to enable the aircraft to fulfil its potential, by keeping it flying at its designated altitude, straight, level and on course. When the whole church is fulfilling its ministry it is achieving its potential. This is the long haul. Equipping and releasing church members into ministry requires long-term commitment, but when each member realizes his or her purpose, and works together for the overall purposes of the church, then the church begins to have an impact on the community.

Every minister's dream is to mobilize the congregation into action. The question is how to do it.

> Chances are that many God-gifted people in your church have not yet reached their potential. As a result, a ripened harvest awaits capable leaders who mobilise their lay people to 'go and make disciples of all nations'.[1]

---

[1] Carl F. George with Warren Bird, *How to Break Growth Barriers*, Baker Book House 1993, p. 163.

Paul stressed that the task of church leaders is to equip people:

> It was he [Christ] who gave some to be apostles, some to be prophets, some to be evangelists, and some to be pastors and teachers, to prepare God's people for works of service, so that the body of Christ may be built up . . . (Ephesians 4:11–12)

But turning members into ministers is a time-consuming task. Most leaders, particularly clergy, find themselves caught up in a multitude of other tasks. They are expected to be effective preachers, and frequent visitors of people in the community as well as in the church. They are expected to attend all the committee meetings, represent the church in denominational responsibilities, be a leader in the local community, meet with church leaders of other traditions, be good administrators, take part in school assemblies, speak at various functions, always be available, spend a lot of time in prayer and study, and discover the gifts and abilities of all the congregation! When regional church leaders, bishops, superintendents and moderators ask a church what kind of ministry they want, the answer is frequently, 'Someone who will identify the gifts of the membership.' In most churches this is far more than one leader can be expected to achieve without disappointing many of the expectations of the congregation and parish.

Pastors and ministers find themselves caught up in frustration believing their members are simply complacent, indifferent and apathetic. It may be nearer the truth that people are just unsure of how to get involved. Also in a larger church it is easy for church members to think there are plenty of other people to do the work – a vicious circle for both congregation and leaders.

Thom Rainer, Dean of the Billy Graham School of Missions, Evangelism and Church Growth at The Southern Baptist Theological Seminary in Louisville, Kentucky, points out that 'The contribution of the Church Growth Movement to the unleashing of the laity is its constant, pragmatic questioning of "how?"'. It is not enough to affirm the biblical principle of lay ministry; we must find ways of equipping people for their tasks.

Greg Ogden identifies six major paradigm shifts since 1960 which have helped the people of God to do the ministry of God.

First, there is a renewed understanding of the role of the Holy Spirit. The third Person of the Trinity is more than a propositional truth; he is the living God who encounters the people of God.

Second, Christianity is now more than an institutional faith for many believers. To be a Christian means to have Christ in us, a moment-by-moment awareness that Christ resides in our lives, empowers us, directs us, and loves through us.

Third, the church is becoming people-focused rather than pastor-focused. The church is being understood as a living organism, in which all the people (pastors and laity alike) contribute to the body of Christ. The renewal of small groups is a visible sign of this new mindset. In this setting, Christians are no longer the audience; they are contributing participants in ministry.

Fourth, a new awareness that all God's people are ministers has caused increased emphasis on discovery and using spiritual gifts.

Fifth, a new ecumenical movement has emerged, a movement transcending denominational loyalties. This movement focuses on reaching the lost and releasing Christians to answer their God-given call to the ministry. This evangelical, ecumenical spirit can most likely find its initial impetus under the leadership of Billy Graham, who provided the direction and resources for the International Congress on World Evangelisation at Lausanne, Switzerland in 1974.

Sixth, the direction of worship has undergone such change that the worship event is, in the minds of some, a new Reformation itself. Worship is shifting from a setting of performance with only the 'actors' participating, to a setting of participation, where all of God's people direct their hearts to God.

This new Reformation is not a foregone conclusion in many churches. In order for the new Reformation to become reality, new roles for both the pastor and the people must be accepted.[2]

This becomes a challenging point of growth. Both leaders and people may find this change of roles painful. Thom Rainer explains that a pastor must be willing to make three major changes in order to fulfil his or her role as an equipper. 'These changes are often painful; for most pastors and laity alike, they are fundamentally different from "the way we've always done it".'[3]

First, leaders must realize that they are the beginning of the necessary change. It is easier to manage this change if you are in a team of full-time church leaders than if you are a solo minister. Even so, the change can only begin with the minister or team leader, whatever your situation.

Second, the minister or team leader must abandon what Ogden calls 'the dependency model', in which the pastor feels the pressure of the congregation to be omnicompetent. Some leaders adopt this dependency model out of a feeling of guilt, others because it strokes their ego. We have to ask if we are willing to be behind-the-scenes equippers who have little recognition. The leader who is willing to let go of this dependency model must be prepared to face criticism and resistance from the members. Rick Warren tells members to let go of their ministers and the ministers to let go of the ministry.

Third, there has to be a change from the dependency model to the equipper model. This, as I have said, is the long haul. It takes a great deal of patience, energy and persistence to lead people to this new model.

---

[2] Greg Ogden, *The New Reformation: Returning the Ministry to the People of God*, Zondervan 1990, quoted in Thom S. Rainer, *The Book of Church Growth*, Broadman 1993, pp. 196–7.
[3] Rainer, *The Book of Church Growth*, p. 198.

9.2 Begin to equip members

Every church needs an intentional process by which to identify, mobilize and support the ministries of its members. Not only must we discover people's giftedness, we must find ways to help them use their gifts, and then support them in their ministries. These three stages are vital if we are to unleash the ministry of church members: identify, mobilize and support. In too many churches the process stops at identification.

Preaching about gifts and every-member ministry is of course one of the primary ways of beginning this process of change. A long period of education helps members to rethink ministry. Church members, however, need not only to be taught and encouraged, they also need to be shown *how* and *where* they can serve. In addition to the teaching and encouragement that comes from the pulpit and Bible study groups, more precise methods of preparing God's people are needed.

Over the years I have used a number of ways to help people know their gifting. I have never been entirely satisfied with any of them. We have tried some of the many questionnaires that are recommended by various para-church organizations. None of them has been very effective in moving members into ministry. They seem to stop short at the 'discovery' stage. 'I've discovered my gift, now what do I do with it?' is the plight of too many Christians.

We now strongly encourage church members to find the time to attend a course on ministry. As with our other specialist small groups, this one meets once a week for eight weeks. We call it 'Ministry Matters'. We teach it three times a year. Throughout the course we teach a biblical approach to ministry. We encourage people prayerfully to discover their gifts, skills and abilities, and the ministry they believe God is calling them to, either in the church, the workplace, or both. The course may lead some people into a full-time vocational ministry in another part of the world.

At the end of each course we use a placement process. We already had a placement scheme for those God is calling to full-time ministry. We interviewed candidates for full-time ministry and mission and worked with mission agencies, Bible and theological colleges to find placements. We also provided support groups for our missionaries, and young people on short-time mission. So we decided also to adopt a placement process for those who are called to stay in the home church and minister there, or through their church, in the workplace. After completing our course on ministry, each person fills in a personal profile and is interviewed by a current church leader.

9.3 Using the acronym SHAPE

Throughout the course we use the SHAPE model, developed years ago by Rick Warren to explain five elements that determine a person's ministry. Each one of us is 'shaped' by God. In the Old Testament, the prophet Jeremiah describes his 'shaping' in these words: 'Before I formed you in the womb I knew you, before you were born I set you apart; I appointed you as a prophet to the nations' (Jeremiah 1:5). We are created by God and he works in each of our lives in various ways.

'S' stands for *spiritual gifts*. We teach what the Bible has to say about gifting. We encourage people to reflect on what gift they may have. At this point they can use a carefully prepared questionnaire. Members are also encouraged to interact with one another and reflect on what others may have observed about their giftedness. Having spent some time on this, we believe this is only one step in the process of discovering what each member believes God has gifted them for.

Many churches find themselves need-driven rather than gift-driven. They have a long list of jobs to be done and spend their time looking for anyone who will fill those vacancies, regardless of gifting. Much energy and time is spent trying to find people simply to do the work that 'needs' to be done. That same energy and time could be used in developing a strategy for becoming a church that uses the gifts of its members to determine its ministries. This will also help to prevent people becoming square pegs in round holes. Somehow you must break out of the vicious circle of being need-driven so that your church can unleash its potential. Discovering the gifting of the membership also guides the church to decide what ministries it should have.

'H' stands for *heart*. Christians talk about having a 'heart' for children, for the elderly, or for some group of people for whom they have a special concern. Some Christians talk about having a 'heart' for a particular country, for a particular race of people, or for an area of the church's ministry. We ask church members on this course, 'Who or what do you think God has given you a heart for?' Jesus said, 'For out of the overflow of the heart the mouth speaks' (Matthew 12:34). The 'heart' represents what we feel passionate about. It is a valid guide to where God wants us to serve.

'A' stands for *abilities*. We all have a set of abilities that we have probably been using for years in many different areas of life. We may have become so used to them that we take them for granted and think they are unimportant. Yet they may be natural abilities and skills that God wants to use and develop. Some abilities may become gifts. We ask people to reflect on how God has used them in their past, or what things they have been good at, even before they became a Christian.

'P' stands for *personality*, or temperament. God has made us all different. Some people are introverts and some are extroverts. Some people love routine, others prefer the freedom of spontaneity. An awareness of our temperament is important as it will determine the way in which our gift will be used. An introvert will use the gift of encouragement in a very different way from an extrovert. Our goal here is to help people towards self-awareness of their own personality, and to reflect on how God may use their giftedness.

'E' stands for life *experiences*. Over the years people will have passed through many different experiences, some painful. Out of these experiences may come a ministry. Paul writes to the Christians in Corinth, 'Praise be to the God of all comfort, who comforts us in all our troubles, so that we can comfort those in any trouble with the comfort we ourselves have received from God' (2 Corinthians 1:3–4). God wants to use the experiences through which we have passed. Years ago, I was deeply impressed and helped by something Bishop Phillips Brooks wrote over a hundred years ago:

> Every new experience is a new opportunity of knowing God. Every new experience is like a jewel set into the texture of our life, on which God shines and makes interpretation and revelation of himself. He wastes nothing. There are some who want to get away from their past. Their life with Christ seems one long failure. But you must learn, you must let God teach you. That the only way to get rid of your past is to get a future out of it. God will waste nothing. There is something in your past, something, even if it only be the sin of which you have repented, which, if you can put it into the Saviour's hands, will be a new life for you.[4]

Exploring these five aspects of development helps each member to understand their 'SHAPE' – the ministry that God has shaped them for. It is not just giftedness that determines ministry. It is the total person. (If you are interested to discover more about SHAPE, read Rick Warren's book.) Warren says:

> You will be most effective and fulfilled in ministry when you use your *spiritual gifts* and *abilities* in the area of your *heart's* desire in a way that best expresses your *personality* and *experiences*.[5]

---

[4] Phillips Brooks, *Phillips Brooks Year Book*, Macmillan 1903.
[5] Rick Warren, *The Purpose-Driven Church*, Zondervan 1995, p. 375.

We have discovered that this approach to helping people into the ministry of the local church has motivated them to get involved. It awakens them to the realization that they do have something to offer. It also helps them to achieve a better balance between the responsibilities of work, home and church. Some of our members have been more motivated to see their work as a place of ministry as well as taking some responsibility in church.

The course is only the beginning. After the one-to-one placement interview we work to find an outlet for each person's ministry. The course will affirm for some that they are already serving where God wants them to serve. For others it will mean a change of direction, while for others it will be the taking up of a new responsibility. We try to match a person's 'SHAPE' to a ministry that already exists in the church, or start a new ministry. Instead of ending up with only a list of vacancies, we also build a list of people ready to serve. It has been thrilling to see the impact of this course on the lives of many individual members and the church as a whole. This is an area where a lot of potential has been released.

With some people we have discovered that there needs to be a period of training. It is vital that people in ministry are nurtured, equipped, supported, and know who they are accountable to. Support not only includes emotional and spiritual support, but also practical support, such as access to office supplies and equipment, teaching materials, and anything that enables them to carry out their ministry.

I have often been asked, 'Where do you find people to lead these groups?' I decided to start at a basic level. First, I personally taught the Newcomers group two or three times until I could pass it over to another leader. I then taught our 'Towards Christian Maturity' group for eight evenings while two of our leaders sat in on it, knowing they would lead it next time. I did the same with 'Ministry Matters'. As I identified future leaders and handed the groups over, I still supported them. It was a process that took two years.

Then came the really exciting part. After 20 members had completed the first 'Ministry Matters', some of these people were ready to take their place in the life of the church. A year later, after three courses had run, we had between 50 and 60 people ready to find their place. We were then creating a pool of people from whom we could draw members into ministry and, as a result of discovering their gifts, some new ministries were emerging as well.

This is surely the principle we see in Acts 6. When the apostles took steps to ensure that certain widows were no longer overlooked 'in the daily distribution of food', they also removed what would have become a hindrance to the continuing growth of the church. The apostles looked for others who could be appointed to this practical ministry, while they continued to exercise 'the ministry of the word'. 'We will turn this responsibility over to them and will give our attention to prayer and the ministry of the word' (Acts 6:3–4). The result? 'So the word of God spread. The number of disciples in Jerusalem increased rapidly, and a large number of priests became obedient to the faith' (Acts 6:7).

If I was still in a church of 70 members, I would now follow this strategy. I believe it is one that can work in almost any sized church. I personally believe that many churches in the UK would greatly benefit from adopting this strategy for involving and equipping members for ministry. If we have learned from others, we hope that others can learn from us. That surely is a New Testament principle for growth.

10

Keep the Church on Course

10.1 Recognize the enemies of growth

Sooner or later, every aircraft pilot learns about drift. The tower clears the aircraft for take-off. The pilot applies full power, lifts smoothly off the runway, and heads for Newcastle. Newcastle is approximately 300 miles north of Biggin Hill. The weather is perfect, the sun is shining, and the pilot steers the plane until it is exactly on course. Having reached the cruise altitude, the pilot settles down to keep a precise compass heading that will take the aircraft all the way to Newcastle.

After an hour of flying time, the pilot begins to look for the town of Skegness, from which the plan is to fly up the east coast to Newcastle. The aircraft is above some low cloud that covers the ground below, but the hope is that this cloud will soon clear. After a while it does, but as the pilot looks down he sees nothing but water! What has happened to the east coast of Britain? Where is it? What has gone wrong? He realizes he is over the North Sea with no land in sight, although he has held carefully to his compass heading. So how has he ended up so far from where he was supposed to be? The answer is that an unseen but powerful force has pushed him slowly out to sea. A 45-mile-an-hour wind from the west has blown the aircraft steadily off course.

124

In a church too we can drift without realizing it. We think we are holding a precise and steady course, but the church may have drifted so far from effective ministry to the community that it has become irrelevant. What unseen force can push a church so far off track?

The Hebrew word *ruach* means 'wind' or 'breath' or 'spirit', depending on the context in which it is used. The Bible talks about evil spirits (winds). The presence of powerful evil influences on our lives is obvious. Satan opposes every church intent on being what God wants it to be. We are in a spiritual battle with a subtle enemy; and it is sometimes hard to discern where he is working until we have drifted so far that it becomes obvious. He uses discouragement to push a church off course.

He uses fear of growth. 'Let's keep the church small' can be a subconscious attitude that prevents a church from fulfilling its potential. A small church is more comfortable and easier to manage, as the members all know each other. In a larger church the force blowing us off track can be complacency. We have a full church. It is easy to settle for 500 members, but there are 15,000 people living within 15 minutes of our church! Our vision can be too small and we can be too quickly satisfied with small gains.

Other forces too push a church off course. One is preoccupation with minor issues. Satan loves nothing more than to get us bogged down in detail and issues other than making disciples. In the hundreds of churches I have visited I have discovered that most churches don't split over big issues. They split over trivia. Most disunity occurs because of minor issues. We are called to 'Make every effort to keep the unity of the Spirit . . .' (Ephesians 4:3). Many churches have been pushed off course and have been diverted from mission and ministry through their preoccupation with minor issues.

Another subtle force is the desire to wait until everybody is spiritually perfect. 'We're not ready to reach out to the community. We need to bring ourselves before God. We've got to set our own house in order first. We have to seek renewal.' These are all very good desires, but sadly they sometimes become an excuse for inaction. It is easier to focus on spiritual renewal than to engage in mission. But by engaging in mission renewal often comes. Over the years I have heard people say, 'We need to finish the building' or 'We need to sort out relationships.' That's fine, except two, three, five, or even ten years later they're still saying the same things.

Then there is a reluctance to accept people who are different from ourselves. I remember lovingly challenging a church member to invite her neighbour to church. She replied: 'Oh, I don't think we want that kind of person in our church!' On another occasion when a local church was reflecting that it had no youth, someone suggested ways of reaching out to young people. The minister responded with 'That's if we want them.' And that wasn't said contemptuously, humorously, or patronizingly – it was a true sentiment!

Another unseen force is 'clinging to tradition', knowingly or unknowingly. We may be unaware that we speak in a different language from the unchurched. A counter-culture is one thing – and the church is called to be that – but not connecting to the prevailing culture is something else. This is not simply about traditional forms of worship – they can work effectively if they are done well, as I have already indicated. My concern is that we can sometimes develop a traditional mindset that in the modern world of leisure and the workplace makes Christians appear irrelevant.

Fear of growth is a very powerful force pushing many churches off track. This fear comes in all sorts of guises. There is the fear that existing church members won't be able to relate to increasing numbers of new people. They may fear losing 'ownership' of the church – 'we like things the way they are' – or being unable to find enough leaders and helpers. And there is the fear that 'we have gone far enough!' I have met this a number of times. On one occasion, after a new church building was completed, the suggestion was made to build a link-block to the older building – a church hall on the same piece of land. The church was growing and more space was needed. But having only just recently completed the new building, and paid for it, people wanted to rest and to feel that the task was finished. It took a change of leadership to continue the vision. It is natural for churches to grow, so we should encourage them to, and not stop them.

Fear is a powerful force. There is a haunting chapter in John Pollock's biography of Billy Graham. Having told the story of the mid-twentieth-century crusades in London and Scotland, John Pollock includes a chapter called 'And Fear to Launch Away'. He writes:

> In the prevailing religious indifferences of the early fifties, which the crusades had done much to shatter, any advance seemed notable; and it did not become evident until the end of the decade how much England lost through the hesitation of those in high places who failed to maintain the momentum generated by the events of 1954–55, but drew back, belittling or doubting the validity of what had happened. . . . Bishop Hugh Gough summed up in 1959. 'To be honest, I think we missed what God intended for us. Many in the Church doubted and even opposed, and as a result I fear the words must be spoken of this country, "Thou knewest not the time of thy visitation."'[1]

This is not the only time the church has failed to seize the moment. It happens in local churches too. The unseen but powerful forces of fear, mistrust, pride and tradition blow the church off God's intended course for it.

Another unseen force is the belief that growth happens only when the message is compromised. Some people assume that in

---

[1] John Pollock, *Billy Graham*, McGraw-Hill 1966, pp. 158–9.

larger churches the leadership is shallow and lacking in theological commitment. Quality is better than quantity, it is said. This can be an irrational excuse, a belief hatched in hell to divert a church from its purpose. There are some churches only interested in numerical growth, but that need not stop us asking God for both quantity and quality. Rick Warren reminds us that 'an exclusive focus on either quality or quantity will produce an unhealthy church. Don't be fooled by either/or thinking.'[2]

It's always easier to say what's wrong with churches than to suggest a way forward. There are many books on diagnosing sickness and fewer on steps to take towards health. A pilot has to take four basic steps in order to keep an aircraft from being blown off course.

Step 1. The pilot must accept the reality of the wind as a real danger, even though it can't be seen. Satan is a real enemy of the church who will do everything in his ability to distract and divert a church from its purpose. We need to be constantly alert. We are in a spiritual battle and we need to be sensitive to the subtle strategies of the enemy and identify them as soon as they appear on the horizon. Be alert to the slow spread of discouragement, a creeping preoccupation with minor issues, a negative or critical attitude, a complacent attitude towards the unchurched, a lack of purpose, and misplaced priorities. These are all schemes of the enemy to be defeated.

Step 2. The pilot must determine the direction from which the wind comes, and also its strength. The Bible tells us that as human beings we naturally tend to be 'blown here and there by every wind of teaching and by the cunning and craftiness of men in their deceitful scheming' (Ephesians 4:14). We need to

---

[2] Rick Warren, *The Purpose-Driven Church*, Zondervan 1995, p. 51.

discover the direction from which this force is coming and face up to it, even if we must acknowledge that its greatest source is often from within ourselves. It may be pride, jealousy, envy, egotism, one-upmanship, complacency, or selfish desires, disguised as wise or good advice from church members claiming to be biblical or 'having a word from the Lord'. It may be a reluctance to give that causes someone to speak against a new project or ministry initiative. It may also come from outside the church in the form of cultural influences or worldly advice.

Step 3. The pilot must correct the aircraft's course by turning the plane into the wind sufficiently to make good the intended course over the ground. In other words, we need to deal with whatever is pushing the church off course. However, once the devil sees we have made the necessary course corrections, he changes the force and the direction of his ill wind. But the church belongs to Christ. We need to keep in daily communion with Christ to constantly make course corrections and defeat the ever-changing patterns and forces of Satan's ill wind, and stay on track. The spiritual health of the church is all-important. We need regular health-checks by measuring our purposes, lifestyles and achievements against biblical principles and values.

Step 4. The pilot must constantly stay alert to the need for further possible course corrections, because a change in wind direction, or wind force, or both, demands a new course. We live in a rapidly changing world. There are frequent cultural changes that push the church off course, making it irrelevant and ineffective. The church constantly needs to assess where it is going, who it is trying to reach, and how it is going to reach them. We must always be alert to the direction in which the Holy Spirit is moving. He continually leads into new spheres, ways and means of spreading the gospel. Society changes; so must the church's methods of reaching society. To fail to do so is to miss God's purpose for the church, which is to communicate dynamically to its time and generation. Yet we must not change the gospel or the basic principles at the core of the Christian faith.

Maintaining course is only part of the pilot's task in keeping an aircraft flying towards its intended destination. *Keeping* the power on is vital. The power of the Holy Spirit is released through prayer. Prayer expresses our dependence on God who alone energizes the church and enables it to fulfil its potential.

Pray and Plan for Growth

11

Prayer: The Power Behind the Principles

A pilot must not only apply the power, but also understand something of its nature. The syllabus for learning to fly includes information about how the engine – the power supply – works, and how to maintain it. Prayer is the power source behind the growth of the church in the book of Acts. We read that before Pentecost 'they all joined together constantly in prayer'. After Pentecost they still continued to pray, with startling results. 'With great power the apostles continued to testify to the resurrection of the Lord Jesus, and much grace was upon them all' (Acts 4:33), and 'more and more men and women believed in the Lord and were added to their number' (Acts 5:14). There is a strong relationship between prayer and church growth.

In Acts 12:5 we read: 'So Peter was kept in prison, but the church was earnestly praying to God for him.' Commenting on that verse, John Stott says:

> Here then were two communities, the world and the church, arrayed against one another, each wielding an appropriate weapon. On the one side was the authority of Herod, the power of the sword and the security of the prison. On the other side, the church turned to prayer, which is the only power which the powerless possess.[1]

---

[1] John R.W. Stott, *The Spirit, the Church, and the World*, IVP 1990.

Prayer was at the heart of church life in Acts. They prayed before they selected and appointed leaders. They prayed during times of persecution. They prayed for the progress of the gospel. They prayed for the ill. They prayed for church leaders and workers. They prayed for the church, and they prayed for the community and the world.

Prayer demonstrates our dependence on God. Even after Pentecost the church showed its dependence on God through prayer. We cannot build churches in our own strength. We might be able to build organizations and institutions, but only God can build the church. If we neglect prayer, we neglect the power source behind all church health and growth.

When Peter Wagner began researching the spiritual dimensions of churches he was led to a much deeper understanding of the role of prayer in church growth.[2] By 1992 he had published three books on the subject. George Barna, in his study of some rapidly growing churches in America, also found that prayer was the foundational ministry of these churches that emphasized prayer in at least four major areas.

First, church members were given consistent biblical teaching about the importance of prayer in the Christian life. Teaching in sermons and the various programmes and ministries of the church encouraged prayer. There was little doubt in the mind of the average church member that prayer was a priority.

Second, the church leaders, beginning with the pastor, modelled dynamic prayer lives. Large segments of time were devoted to prayer despite busy schedules. Some pastors spent more time praying about their sermons than preparing them.

Third, the rapidly growing churches learned that praise for answered prayer was an integral part of prayer itself. The

[2] C. Peter Wagner, *How to Have a Healing Ministry Without Making Your Church Sick*, Regal 1987.

people learned that prayer really is effective as they heard about the many answers.

Fourth, growing churches engendered accountability for prayer. The prayer life of members, the prayer ministries of the church, and the prayer life of church leaders were regularly held before the church.[3]

Prayer is indispensable to understanding God's vision for churches. Not only must we look beyond the world's ideas for vision, we must look beyond the visions of other churches. Though we can certainly learn from other growing churches, the vision God gives to one church is not the same as He gives to another church. As we pray to God for a vision for our churches, He will miraculously open our eyes to possibilities.[4]

The prayers of the early church unleashed the power of God to add thousands to the church. It happened then. It is happening in churches today. And it can happen in your church.[5]

Pray for spiritual and numerical growth. It is God's will for his church to be healthy, and a healthy church will attract people.

11.1 Leaders must set the pace

Put prayer at the heart of leaders' meetings at every level. Evaluate your own prayer life, and put prayer at the centre of the leaders' own personal lives. Make time for larger prayer periods on the agenda of elders' and deacons' meetings, PCCs and pastoral leaders' meetings. Encourage significant periods of prayer at the meetings of children's workers and youth workers, at the various team conferences and committees of all

[3] George Barna, *User Friendly Churches*, Regal 1991.
[4] Thom S. Rainer, *The Book of Church Growth*, Broadman 1993, p. 178.
[5] *Ibid.*, p. 184.

groups in the life of the church. Prayer needs to characterize not only worship planning, but every aspect of the church's ministry. Make prayer in all small groups part of their corporate experience, inviting group members to participate. Handle it sensitively, showing care towards those who are not yet ready to pray openly. Allow people to stay silent until they feel comfortable about praying in front of others.

11.2 Teach the value and effectiveness of prayer

The pulpit is a powerful tool for demonstrating and teaching the effectiveness of prayer, to both believers and unbelievers, and small groups are even better for discovering the power of prayer. Encourage the church by telling the members how prayers have been answered for specific events in the life of the church. Help people to tell their own stories of answered prayer. Build confidence in prayer through teaching and testimony.

In larger congregations, use prayer carefully during worship. Charles Spurgeon counselled his students in his *Lectures on Preaching* not to pray for long periods of time in public worship services. Most Christians admit that sustaining concentration during long prayers in worship is difficult, even more so for people not used to church. Seeker-sensitive worship needs to use prayer sparingly. Larger congregations of believers can break into small groups for periods of prayer. Smaller congregations can sometimes simply become a prayer meeting! People can be encouraged to pray silently as well as audibly. The size of the congregation often dictates the ways in which people's prayers are integrated into the life of the church. The value, practice and place of prayer needs to be taught at the earliest point of entry into the church. Members need to be taught how to pray, and about the many different forms that prayer can take. Encourage members to find spiritual models that inspire them to pray and prayer partners who help them to pray.

11.3 Set up prayer teams

Rather than use the term 'prayer meetings' for small prayer groups, it may be more helpful to use 'prayer teams'. Set up prayer teams for specific purposes such as special worship services or outreach events. The team idea can be used for all the ongoing ministries in the church. Have a prayer team praying in a small room throughout every worship service. Remember that prayer is engaging in spiritual warfare. Satan will oppose any spiritual and numerical growth that God wants to bless. Prayer is one of the principal weapons in the battle against those powers that try to prevent or slow down the growth of the church. At some point in any plan of church growth, Satan will unleash his forces to frustrate the growth of God's church. As mentioned in the previous chapter, the battle may come from church members whose comfort zone or power niche has been threatened, or the battle may come from outside the church.

Prayer teams can be formed for short- or long-term purposes, for individuals passing through a difficult time or for ongoing needs in the community, nation or world. Use prayer teams as part of the support structures for church members involved in full-time mission in some other part of the world or in the local community.

11.4 Make use of prayer emphases

Give special emphasis at certain times of the year to prayer. Suggest a 24-hour period of prayer and fasting. We have used Good Friday as a day of prayer for the opportunity for spiritual and numerical growth on Easter Sunday. Start a new season's work with a prayer week, suggesting certain times of each day when as many people as possible can meet in groups to pray, or as an entire church. Those in the workplace or in residential homes can also mark those times in practical and appropriate ways.

Have a 'prayer walk' either around the church premises, stopping to pray for the various activities that take place in each room, or around the community, stopping to pray for the people and needs of the area. Be as creative as possible in prayer.

Larger churches often have difficulty in arranging church-wide prayer meetings. Such meetings are often used as a barometer of the church's health, and if poorly attended can be discouraging. However, there should be times when the whole church is called to corporate prayer. We have found one of the best times is at the beginning of the autumn, winter and spring terms. We take an evening and spend some of the time in corporate prayer and some in prayer groups.

Organize a prayer conference, either at a residential centre or in the church. Plan a longer period of prayer, fasting and giving before a major project such as a special building programme, a mission, or the calling of a leader. Above all, pray for the overall health and growth of the church.

Have a plan to increase the level of prayer in the life of the church. Plan a day of prayer. Then sometime later, arrange a week of prayer. In between, focus on teaching and encouraging prayer. Then have a longer sustained period of prayer. Build up the prayer life of the church. Lead the church to seek God and to depend on God for spiritual and numerical growth. It is God's church and he wants it to grow.

An idea has come from South Korea where thousands of people have come to Christ. It's called a 'One, One, One Prayer Movement'. Everyone identifies one non-believer and makes a commitment to pray for one person for one minute at 1 p.m. every day. Give everyone a card with 'One, One, One' on it, to remind them to pray. It's a way of beginning to pray for lost people. One church did this for ten weeks leading up to Easter; or it can be done leading up to any significant outreach event. The value of this is that it gets people started and familiar with praying more frequently for the unchurched. It is something that is do-able!

11.5 Make more of prayer meetings

Give thought to setting aside a room solely for prayer. Encourage church members to give time each week praying over requests listed in the room. The room can also be used during worship services where a prayer team meets.

Pray strategically for people. Pray for one another in the church family, or group. Pray for the leaders of the church. Pray for newcomers to be attracted to the church. Pray for relationships to grow. Pray specifically for people to come to faith in Christ. Even if no one else is praying like this, you can. I remember a Baptist minister who had not seen a baptism in his church for several years. He felt his people were discouraged and unmotivated. They were suspicious of goals. So without saying anything to anyone, he set himself the goal of praying for two people to be baptized within the next couple of months. To his own surprise he baptized four people within that period. He prayed specifically and strategically for the church to grow, and it did.

When a group meets for prayer, it will be more effective if it has some structure. Small groups can be totally spontaneous, but larger groups need a leader. To prevent the 'prayer meeting' becoming aimless or dominated by strong individuals with their own agenda, plan beforehand what kind of 'prayer meeting' it will be. You may want to begin with a time of worship with an emphasis on thanksgiving and praise. Use songs and prayers. Between the songs suggest that people might offer brief prayers of thanksgiving. If a group doesn't find spontaneous prayer easy, have two or three prepared prayers that can be read together displayed on a screen. Encourage the use of the Psalms. Have a period focusing on the need for prayers of confession. Let the group say a prayer together, read David's confession in Psalm 51, and sing a song that celebrates God's forgiveness. Even in a larger church it is encouraging for the whole church to spend some time praying in a group. The larger the group, the more it will need to be structured and led. For the prayers of intercession it is better to break into small groups of six or eight people. Sometimes even a group this size will need a leader if it is a group of people who do not find it easy to pray. You can give each group three or four items to pray about, or provide all the groups with a paper highlighting subjects for prayer.

'Prayer meetings' also provide an opportunity for teaching. Have a 15-minute Bible study to motivate people for prayer. Help people to understand that prayer can involve discipline, effort and hard work. The devil will do everything he can to defeat us. John Earwicker, in his helpful and practical book *Prayer Pace-Setting*, says, 'Prayer is work: working at understanding God's plans; working on co-operating with God's purposes.'[6] John's book is chiefly a resource manual for mobilizing young people in prayer, but contains many helpful practical ideas which can be used among all age groups.

There are many books written calling on Christians to pray for revival. Among them is *Rivers of Renewal* by Neil T. Anderson and Elmer L. Towns (Regal 1997). Ronald Dunn's book *Don't Just Stand There . . . Pray Something* (Alpha 1991) concentrates on intercessory prayer. Most Christians agree on the priority of prayer for that and other purposes. Church leaders, hopefully, do not need convincing of its importance. So why isn't it happening on a larger scale? Busy lives, many distractions, lack of focus, lack of discipline and lack of vision may all be contributing factors. All of this reveals the need to teach the principles of prayer early on in the life of a new believer, and for leaders to set the pace in leading the whole church to become a praying church.

On the outside we may look like a non-praying church, but behind the crowds of seekers and all that is public and visible

---

[6] John Earwicker, *Prayer Pace-Setting*, Scripture Union 1987, p. 91.

about a growing church there will be a committed core of praying believers: individuals, prayer partners, prayer teams, prayer support groups, in addition to those occasions when as many believers as possible come together to be the church at prayer. Prayer needs to be a highly visible part of a healthy church to believers, but it may be invisible in the main to unbelievers until they come to faith.

The theologian and teacher Dr Paul Tillich once said:

The church is potentially a powerful body with a necessary arsenal at its disposal to change the moral character of this world. The fact that it is not doing so causes us to be painfully aware that its potential is not being realised. That which is possible is not being produced, for while possessing the dynamite of the Gospel, the church has lost its detonator (explosiveness). As a result of this inaction, the church that the world sees is weak, timid, divided, and crawling instead of flying. While it has material resources to convert the world, it is restricted by its stinginess and narrowness of vision.

12

Planning – Putting the Principles to Work

The success of nearly every flight depends on the preparation of a clear flight plan. Before the aircraft leaves the ground, the pilot will fill out a flight plan, showing the various compass headings, flight levels, and check points along the way. Even when the pilot flies around the airfield, the 'pattern' or 'circuit', those four legs of the rectangle need to be clear in his or her mind. He or she needs to know the direction the aircraft should be travelling, the turning points, and the correct levels at each stage of the circuit.

Few churches have a flight plan. Christian Schwarz points out that 'Natural church development is not a strategy to create spiritual momentum. It comes in where spiritual momentum already exists and shows practical steps to attract more and more people.'[1]

In other words, the church needs to plan as well as pray. Prayer alone will not make a church grow. Rick Warren says:

Some of the greatest prayer warriors I know are pastors and members of dying churches. Of course, prayer is absolutely essential. A prayerless ministry is a powerless ministry. But it takes far

---

[1] Christian Schwarz, *Natural Church Development*, Church Smart Resources 1996, p. 107.

more than prayer to grow a church. It takes skilled action. One time God told Joshua to stop praying about his failure and get up and correct the cause of it instead (Joshua 7). There is a time to pray, and there is a time to act responsibly. We must always be careful to avoid two extreme positions in ministry. One extreme is to assume all responsibility for the growth of the church. The other extreme is to abdicate all responsibility for it.[2]

David Porter, Director of ECONI (Evangelical Contribution on Northern Island) speaking in March 1999, said that in Northern Ireland evangelical Christians reached a point where they felt that prayer was not enough. They needed to get out and be peacemakers.

Some Christians think we should not plan because it is unspiritual. They are sceptical about applying practical principles of church health and growth, even if those principles are biblically based. They are sceptical even of the words 'church growth'. I understand that. It seems simplistic and worldly, as if people are trying to do things in their own strength. Indeed there is a kind of church growth thinking that ignores the Holy Spirit and has negatively influenced many people against planning and applying principles. Consequently, they are afraid of setting goals. An overemphasis on numerical growth has made many Christians nervous and sceptical. Criticism of some aspects of the church growth movement has been justifiable. However, that doesn't mean to say that numerical growth is neither desirable nor biblical.

Schwarz says:

Church growth in the power of the Holy Spirit does not mean ignoring God's principles. It means putting those principles to work in our churches as much as possible, even when they seem unusual, hard to follow, go against our tradition, or even hurt.[3]

---

[2] Rick Warren, *The Purpose-Driven Church*, Zondervan 1995, p. 58.
[3] Schwarz, *Natural Church Development*, p. 126.

To be lost in an aircraft is frightening. Even if you can see the ground you may not recognize familiar landmarks and so become confused and afraid. It happened once to me and it was one of the most terrifying moments of my life. Similarly, for a church to be lost in terms of its direction and purpose breeds division, frustration and fear.

Our plans need to come from God. Some people worry that planning precludes the sovereignty of God and the leadership of the Holy Spirit. On the contrary. Prayer, dependence on the Holy Spirit and careful reading of Scripture will reveal God's plans for the church. The fact is that churches that plan for growth usually experience growth. Peter Wagner lists six reasons for planning:[4]

1. It increases efficiency. God's resources of time, energy and money are best used for good stewardship.
2. It permits mid-course corrections.
3. It unites the team with a singular plan and vision. Each member of the team understands his or her role in the vision.
4. It helps measure effectiveness. Progress is measured according to the plans.
5. It makes accountability natural.
6. It can become a model to help others.

The Bible supports planning: 'those who plan what is good find love and faithfulness' (Proverbs 14:22). The story of Nehemiah rebuilding the wall of Jerusalem includes his careful planning as well as his praying. Jesus said:

> Suppose one of you wants to build a tower. Will he not first sit down and estimate the cost to see if he has enough money to complete it? For if he lays the foundation and is not able to finish it, everyone who sees it will ridicule him, saying, 'This fellow began to build and was not able to finish.' (Luke 14:28–30)

---

[4] Peter Wagner, *Strategies for Church Growth*, Regal 1987, pp 32–34.

In 1 Corinthians 9 we see an example of planning by the apostle Paul.

God himself is a planner. Some Christians use the phrase 'the plan of salvation'. Early in the ministry of Jesus, when the disciples found him in a solitary place and said 'Everyone is looking for you!', Jesus replied,

> Let us go somewhere else – to the nearby villages – so that I can preach there also. That is why I have come.' So he travelled throughout Galilee, preaching in their synagogues and driving out demons. (Mark 1:37–9)

Jesus would not be diverted from his mission.

Strategies for spiritual and numerical growth that focus on building up the health of the church may sound businesslike. They may not be biblical in the literal sense, but they are biblical in that they derive their inspiration and motivation from the Bible and are based on God's desire for his church to grow. 'The tools of planning and goal-setting can be of tremendous benefit. They can be steps of faith; but they must be guided carefully by the hand of God.'[5]

12.1 Ask key questions of your church

All four churches I have had the privilege to lead had planned growth. How did we go about it? We began by asking questions like the following:

1.   What is the essential purpose of the church and how does it relate to our congregation and community?
2.   How should this purpose affect the aims and plans of the church, and does it actually do so?
3.   Therefore, what should be the aims of the congregation?

---

[5] Thom S. Rainer, *The Book of Church Growth*, Broadman 1993, p. 270.

4. Are the church members conscious of these aims? If not, why not?
5. Do these aims govern the development of the church, its organizations and their functions? If not, why not?
6. Are there definite long-, mid- and short-term growth goals?
7. Are the goals measurable and attainable?
8. Are the goals and aims connected to the purpose of the church?

Before taking these questions to the whole church, the leadership needs to reflect on them. In a solo ministry, there might be opposition to this approach. If so, don't be put off as the minister in charge to address these questions in your own mind. If the minister has no goals and aims that fit the purpose of the church there will be little progress in building up the health and growth of the church. However, if the minister is the only one who has some goals that are measurable and attainable, he or she can eventually change the direction of the church. Change often begins on a small scale, with pastors setting a few simple aims for their own lives and the way in which, as leaders, they lead the church. I remember in my first church simply asking God to help me bring fresh energy and life to the Sunday morning worship services over a number of months. No one knew I had set that goal. They simply saw the change. I knew that God had answered prayer and was honoured by efforts to achieve what I believed was his purpose.

On other occasions I have set the goal of building up Sunday evening congregations. In all four churches the attendance at the evening meetings was considerably less than at the morning ones. I asked myself, 'Why do we have an evening congregation? Who is it for? What does it achieve? What should be its purpose?' It seemed to me that an evening worship service should not be a repeat format of a morning service. I have also discovered that there are people who much prefer evening attendance. Should we provide for them, and if so, how? Having answered these and other questions I decided to keep planning a series of evening services that contained special items. We deliberately planned to invite musicians or speakers not included in the mornings, and moved to a more informal approach. For the past 20 years I have witnessed growing attendances in our evening congregations. This is clearly against the trend in many churches. As I write, last Sunday evening we had a congregation of approximately 350. That is not huge, but for a local church in a small community, it is encouraging.

I start with a personal goal that isn't always obvious to others. Nehemiah said at one moment in his planning strategy, 'I had not told anyone what my God had put in my heart to do for Jerusalem' (Nehemiah 2:12). There comes a time to share a goal so that it is taken up and owned by the people so that it becomes their goal too.

Planning for growth starts with a change of attitude on the part of the leaders. I expected our evening worship services to grow and my sense of expectation was sensed and shared. Attitudes are contagious and are powerful. It is therefore important to have constructive attitudes. A good place to begin is to adopt the ten practical goals mentioned in Chapter 3.

12.2 Survey the community

Having set a few basic goals and aims, take a longer look at the surrounding community. There are a number of helpful community surveys you could choose. One is included in the *Making Sunday Best* resource pack produced by Fanfare 2000. The following steps are reproduced here with permission.

1. Prepare a map of the community showing the area considered to be the church's responsibility.
2. Describe the area – type of housing, age of population,

racial patterns, general culture, subcultural groups, income level, educational level, problems related to the environment. The demographics of the area are vital to have. Discover the future of the community as well as the present.
3. Describe the community needs that should be met by the church.
4. Evaluate the effectiveness of the church in meeting the needs of the community. What can and should be done to meet those needs? What future needs can be anticipated and prepared for?

12.3 Survey the church

Take a good long look at the present state of the church. Summarize briefly its history and how this relates to the present congregational life. Evaluate and criticize the church's constitution and/or bye-laws if it has any. Study the church property and buildings. How adequate are the buildings and resources to meet the needs of the community? Are the present buildings used to the best advantage in accordance with the church's message and ministry?

Continue the survey to look at the worship life of the church, its pastoral care, education and teaching processes. Describe the outreach ministry of the church. What is actually being done in terms of evangelism and world mission? Are the worship services effectively evangelistic? What recreational and social ministries are there?

Much more needs to be done, but it is obvious that the purpose of such surveys is the assessment of the total life of the church and its impact on the community with a view to growth and kingdom extension.

Plan to be a healthy church:

That comes through a process of comparison, consultation, and self-evaluation. Comparison is made with other churches, especially healthy ones. Consultations with outsiders help us to see ourselves as others see us. Self-evaluation is applying insider's insights to the comparison and consultations.[6]

12.4 Set quality goals

Christian Schwarz in his helpful book *Natural Church Development* gives examples of qualitative goals. He says:

> Qualitative goals are precise, time-bound, verifiable, measurable goals which relate to the *increase of quality in a church*. It is not a 'qualitative goal' when a church member says, 'I want to be a better Christian,' or when a church declares, 'In the future we want to relate to each other in a more loving and spiritual way.' These are nice statements, but they are not goals.

He then lists eight examples of qualitative goals in the areas of ministry: leadership, spirituality, structures, worship, small groups, evangelism and relationships. Each goal has a time period. For example, under 'spirituality' he suggests, 'By February 1 we will have decided which of the three lay workers under consideration will assume co-ordination of the prayer ministry.' Under 'worship' he says, 'From the beginning of next year, we will have a worship service each quarter which is specifically designed to reach non-Christians.' Under 'evangelism' he says, 'By the end of April the church leadership will have identified some of the Christians God has blessed with the gift of evangelism and will have had a personal conversation with each one regarding this gift.'

---

[6] Leith Anderson, *A Church for the Twenty-First Century*, Bethany House 1992, p. 128.

13

Signs of a Healthy Church

13.1 It glorifies God

A healthy church is one that draws attention to the true character of God. For many people their understanding of the
character of God is directly tied to the character of the local
church. Churches that are welcoming, compassionate, support-
ive, seeking to serve rather than be served, coping with relationships in a Christian manner, are churches that glorify God.
In some people's eyes, God has a poor reputation because the
church has let him down. He is thought of as harsh, unloving,
inconsiderate, prejudiced, uncaring and unapproachable. Just
as the individual Christian's life can affect a person's understanding of God, so can the worship and ministry of a local
church community. What do people think of when they pass by
your church? Might they regard it as self-centred, arrogant or
uncaring? A healthy church is more concerned about drawing
and attracting attention to the true character of God – glorify-
ing God – than about looking after its own organization, representing the denomination to which it belongs, or guarding its
own way of doing things.

13.2 It keeps the unity of the Spirit

Ephesians 4 stresses the importance of unity in the body of Christ. The church is not an organization, it is an organism. It is a body, a family of people drawn together by their relationship with God. 'Be completely humble and gentle; be patient, bearing with one another in love. Make every effort to keep the unity of the Spirit through the bond of peace' (Ephesians 4:2–3). The 'effort' is honouring to Christ and it is attractive to the world. A sign of health is when Christians cope with conflict creatively and constructively, when they embrace the core values of forgiveness and reconciliation, and as Ephesians 4:31 goes on to say:

> Get rid of all bitterness, rage and anger, brawling and slander, along with every form of malice. Be kind and compassionate to one another, forgiving each other, just as in Christ God forgave you.

13.3 It provides a place to grow

Unity implies fellowship. Christianity is relational. One of our church members, Jacquie Moyse, a Christian counsellor, described the church as being a place where people can grow spiritually, emotionally and relationally. She said:

> The church is often far from being the growth facilitating place one might expect. This is often the result of 'unbalanced' theological teaching taught and applied by insecure church leadership. Often this is met with confused understanding in the church member, and unawareness of negative transferences and counter transferences that may be in play. These factors together can aggravate the problems with which individuals enter the church and sometimes are the cause of problems of those reared in families called 'Christian', effectively stunting growth.

Jacquie asks the question 'What is 'growth?' and answers as follows:

I see growth as marked by the following factors in the individual: The freedom to put away pretence, and to be relaxed about how one appears in the sight of others; to grow the ability to put aside the negative inner sense of duty that sometimes arises from those who would impose obligations upon others; to grow toward being able to make decisions and act upon them; to gain respect for self and others; to move toward valuing the experience of the moment, the fact of 'being' rather than always striving to meet targets of achievement; to discover freedom for feelings to be valued and acknowledged, whether positive or negative, seeing these as valuable aspects of the whole person; to learn to value trust and intimacy in relationship.

13.4 It incorporates newcomers

The way newcomers are welcomed and incorporated into the community of the local church is one of the most identifiable signs of health in a church. Leith Anderson says, 'Healthy churches assimilate new people into the life and leadership of the congregation.'[1] He goes on to say:

One way to check the health of the assimilation process is to listen to how long it takes newcomers to switch their pronouns from your church and their church to our church and my church. Healthy churches incorporate new people as equal members in a short enough period of time that those people do not become discouraged and go elsewhere.[2]

13.5 It makes disciples

It is God's will for his church to grow. Colossians 1:6 says: 'All over the world this gospel is bearing fruit and growing, just as

---

[1] Leith Anderson, *A Church for the Twenty-First Century*, Bethany House 1992, p.135.
[2] *Ibid.*, p. 137.

it has been doing among you since the day you heard it and understood God's grace in all its truth.' Colossians 2:19 describes how 'the whole body, supported and held together by its ligaments and sinews, grows as God causes it to grow', while Paul writes to Timothy that God 'wants all men to be saved and to come to a knowledge of the truth' (1 Timothy 2:4).

Numerical and spiritual growth are clearly God's purpose for his church. It is not just increasing attendance on Sundays, however; it is making disciples by incorporating them into the church family.

In Matthew 28:19–20 Jesus gives clear instructions to his disciples. He wants the people who become disciples, are baptized and taught, to grow. In Acts 1:8 the vision is clarified and strengthened: 'But you will receive power when the Holy Spirit comes on you; and you will be my witnesses in Jerusalem, and in all Judea and Samaria, and to the ends of the earth.' In Acts 2:39, 41; 4:4; 6:1 we see the outworking of that vision. In Acts 9:31 we read: 'Then the church throughout Judea, Galilee and Samaria enjoyed a time of peace. It was strengthened; and encouraged by the Holy Spirit, it grew in numbers, living in the fear of the Lord.' Here is growth on all fronts – spiritual and numerical, quality and quantity. Charles Haddon Spurgeon, the famous pastor/evangelist of the late nineteenth century argues:

I am not among those who decry statistics, nor do I consider that they are productive of all manner of evil; for they do much good if they are accurate, and if men use them lawfully. It is a good thing for people to see the nakedness of the land through statistics of decrease, that they may be driven on their knees before the Lord to seek prosperity; and, on the other hand, it is by no means an evil thing for workers to be encouraged by having some account of results set before them. I should be very sorry if the practice of adding up, and deducting, and giving in the net result were to be abandoned, for it must be right to know our numerical condition. It has been noticed that those who object to the process are often brethren whose unsatisfactory reports should somewhat humiliate them: this is not always so, but it is suspiciously frequent. I heard of the report of a church, the other day, in which the minister, who was well known to have reduced his congregation to nothing, somewhat cleverly wrote, 'Our church is looking up.' When he was questioned with regard to this statement, he replied, 'Everybody knows that the church is on its back and it cannot do anything else but look up.' When churches are looking up in that way, their pastors generally say that statistics are very delusive things, and that they cannot tabulate the work of the Spirit and calculate the prosperity of the church by figures. The fact is, you can reckon very correctly if the figures are honest, and if all circumstances are taken into consideration: if there is no increase, you may calculate with considerable accuracy that there is not much being done; and if there is a clear decrease among a growing population you may reckon that the prayers of the people and the preaching of the minister are not of the most powerful kind.[3]

Healthy churches take to heart the task of making disciples. The Great Commission, Matthew 28:19–20, is important to them. They plan a strategy of outreach into the community. They are concerned and pray hard when no one comes to faith in Christ. They are concerned about those who are 'lost'. They are not content to be the ninety-nine. Disciple-making is exciting, thrilling, inspiring, challenging and transforming for those involved.

---

[3] C. Peter Wagner, *Reporting Church Growth*, 1997, as quoted in *The Soul Winner*, Christian Focus Publications 1992, pp. 17–18.

14

Check the Plan with God's Purpose

All aircraft pilots are aware of vertigo. In aeronautical terms, it
is 'an error or illusion of spatial orientation, an experience in
which the pilot is confused about his [or her] relationship to the
earth or to other objects in the sky'. Pilots aren't the only
victims of vertigo. Birds can experience it as well. Ballet dancers
get vertigo, and so do churches!

Pilots can be under the impression that their aircraft is flying
straight and level in cloud, while in fact they are climbing and
slowing down so dangerously that they could spin out of
control in what could prove to be, if they were near the ground,
a fatal spiral dive. A pilot flying in cloud has to monitor the
flight instruments constantly. It is drummed into the pilot who
flies into cloudy conditions and loses visual reference to the
ground to 'forget everything you think, forget everything you
feel. Concentrate on what those instruments tell you. Believe
them and nothing else and correct your aircraft's flight according to the instruments rather than listen to what your emotions
tell you.'

If a church is to be structured for growth, it must keep its
focus on the instrument panel of God's word. A church that is
not structured in a biblical way is open to dangers such as a
kind of spiritual dictatorship and heavy shepherding or, at the

other extreme, overdemocratic reliance on committee procedure rather than seeking the mind of Christ; on business practice rather than on the Holy Spirit. The tragedy of vertigo is that pilots who have it rarely recognize it, until it's too late. That's why they need to monitor the instruments. A church can lose all sense of direction and purpose unless its structures are constantly reviewed by biblical standards and renewed accordingly.

Thom Rainer, in *The Book of Church Growth*, has a section under the heading 'Restructuring'. In it he says:

> Most churches are not structured for the laity to do ministry. Persons involved in the church often spend their time on committees or boards rather than in front-line ministry. Wagner comments that 'as the church grows it gets more and more unwieldy . . . and tend(s) to multiply boards and committees ad infinitum.' Instead of providing opportunities for ministry, this leaderless structure, says Wagner, 'drags down the church'.[1]

14.1 Structure for growth not control

As the church grows beyond 400 members, the role of its church council – elders, deacons, or PCC – must change. Planning and administration becomes a staff function. A 'council' is essential, but if the church is to continue to grow from 400 to 800, then the pastoral team provides the vision, does the planning and, some would say, even creates the budget.

The team then goes to the church council for approvals and policy. The 'council' comes to understand that the pastoral team provides direction and the 'council' (PCC, or elders or deacons) will provide policy, and everyone else – 95 per cent or more of the church – gets involved in hands-on ministry.

Carl George develops this point in *How to Break Growth*

---

[1] Thom S. Rainer, *The Book of Church Growth*, Broadman 1993, p. 200.

Barriers. He refers to 'board members', by which he means whoever is the governing body or council of the church. In the UK we are familiar with PCCs, and in nonconformist churches, elders and deacons. Whatever we call this governing body, it is vital to understand how its traditional role changes if the church is to continue healthy growth. George says:

> When the church is smaller, board members (meaning church councils) see themselves as the structurally empowered leaders of the church. They want to set the budget, the plan, and the dream. Then they want the paid, professional clergy to carry it out. If a church is to become bigger, the staff must commission ministry and take policy direction from the boards. To grow beyond an attendance of 800 to 1200, a church must have staff-initiated leadership. Too many details arise that cannot wait until the board convenes each month. No matter how efficient the board tries to be, it can regularly bottleneck the staff's efforts to build growth momentum.[2]

The continuing role of the council or governing body should be to authorize policy and establish standard operating procedures. It also acts as a basis for accountability. Governing members, however, must serve as role models for the church. They are to set biblical examples of leadership and spiritual maturity, and help preserve the values that the clergy are seeking to build into the church.

The council should be responsible for appointing senior staff, resolving staff conflicts, and implementing mission and ministry. The church council needs to be part of the active planning process. 'The key is to direct the board's energy and skill into owning and fleshing out the pastor's vision, not wading through the details of implementation.'[3]

---

[2] Carl F. George, *How to Break Growth Barriers*, Baker Book House 1995, pp. 147–9.
[3] *Ibid.*, p. 152.

By the time a church reaches 800 in attendance, the taking of initiative will be the responsibility of the senior staff, rather than a governing body. If all initiatives come from the governing body, it is likely that the church will not grow any larger. It will remain structured for control and not for growth.

In healthy, growing churches the emphasis is much more on people than on structures. These churches think less about their own structures and more about ministry. They emphasize flexibility, simplicity, relationships and functionality. Many churches fail to grow because they are overmanaged and underled.

The larger the church becomes, the more congregational decision-making becomes less practical and more staff-led. This is because in a larger church, decisions are made on a daily, if not hourly, basis. This changes the role of elders, deacons and PCCs which now deal more with overall policy. It is inevitable in a growing church that when it reaches a certain size it becomes more and more staff-led, because for committed Christians not in paid ministry, their first priority is God, their second is their family, the third is their work, and church is only the fourth priority in their life. The church is the place where they worship, where they are part of God's family, and through which they serve, often in the workplace as well as in the church structures. They may be involved in leadership, and that level may be part of the overall policy-making process of the church, but in a busy, growing church, they cannot be involved in the everyday, moment-by-moment decisions.

Each 45 per cent of growth calls for a new structure. 'As church growth moves toward an average attendance of 150, it often slows to a halt simply because the pastor becomes exhausted and incapable of keeping up with all of the expectations.'[4]

In George Barna's *User Friendly Churches*, he explains that

---

[4] Monte Sahlin, *Ministry*, published by Seventh Day Adventists 1997, p. 12.

successful churches 'subscribe to a common philosophy: the ministry is not called to fit the church's structure; the structure exists to further effective ministry'. That means that when the structure doesn't work, it is changed. Barna adds:

> These churches had a keen sense of direction and purpose (i.e., vision and plans). *Their top priority was to achieve their ministry goals.* If the organisational charts and structural procedures inhibited such ministry, they would cautiously but willingly work around the barriers. They were not about to let a man-made system hinder their ability to take advantage of a God-given opportunity to change lives for the Kingdom. Structure, in fact, was not an issue in these churches. Certainly, these congregations were led by individuals who see the wisdom of developing and maintaining orderly processes. They recognised the importance of formal hierarchy of authority, and the importance of avoiding anarchy (even if the intentions of the anarchists are good). *But structure was viewed as a support system, a means to an end, rather than an end in itself.* The structures they used had been developed, accepted, implemented, re-evaluated and upgraded. At all times, the focus was upon ministry, not structure.[5] (Italics mine.)

Avoid the dangers of relying too much on committee procedure rather than seeking the mind of Christ; relying more on business practice than on the Holy Spirit. Don't be afraid to make course corrections in order to stay on track. Constantly review and renew structures according to biblical standards.

14.2 Structure around small groups

Carl F. George in *Prepare Your Church for the Future* says that the church of the future may return to a structure similar to the church in Acts, large enough to attract thousands but small enough to have a personal touch:

---

[5] George Barna, *User Friendly Churches*, Regal 1991, pp. 137–38.

It is my contention that our present models for doing ministry are ineffective and inadequate for the opportunities that are coming our way. If the Christian churches are to receive the harvest of souls that we believe God is calling to enter his kingdom, it will happen only when churches have reorganised their structures. They must be large enough to make a difference and yet small enough to care.[6]

The power of small groups is illustrated by what has happened in China. When the Communists took over control of the country in the 1950s, a period of fierce persecution of the church began. It was feared that the Chinese church might be eliminated. However, over a period of 30 years the Chinese church multiplied 100 times, with estimates of its strength varying between 30 and 100 million people. Small groups were the reason for its survival and growth.

Carl George, Director of the Charles E. Fuller Institute of Evangelism and Church Growth in California, states the case strongly:

> I believe that the smaller group within the whole – called by dozens of terms, including the small group or the cell group – is a crucial but underdeveloped resource in most churches. It is, I contend, the most strategically significant foundation for spiritual formation and assimilation, for evangelism and leadership development, for the most essential functions that God has call for in the church. . . . It's so important that everything else is to be considered secondary to its promotion and preservation.[7]

Small groups, as we have proved in Frinton, are an excellent way to assimilate newcomers and new members into the life and ministry of the church. This can help to satisfy the search for a sense of belonging.

---

[6] Carl F. George, *Prepare Your Church for the Future*, Fleming H. Revell 1991.
[7] *Ibid.*

Build into any small-group structure good leadership and accountability. In Exodus 18:13–23 Moses' father-in-law, Jethro, advised him to set up a small-group structure to meet the needs of the Israelites. Jethro organized each of the two million Israelites into groups of ten with a leader placed over each group. A leader of 50 was then placed over five other group leaders. Next there were leaders of 100, then finally leaders of 1,000. This kind of structure encourages the identification and appointment of leaders and establishes a system of accountability.

An example of the effectiveness of small groups is given by Thom Rainer. He quotes the New Hope Community Church in Portland, Oregon, which began in 1972:

> The most rapid growth came after the tenth anniversary of the church. From 1982 to 1990 membership increased by four thousand members. The key to the growth has been the outreach of about five hundred small groups. The threefold purpose of the TLC (tender loving care) groups is discipling, evangelising, and shepherding. The cell-group system began with one group for every ten members. By 1990, 4,800 persons were in weekly attendance in 485 groups. The one-to-ten ratio has remained constant for nearly 20 years. New Hope Community Church uses five levels: lay people, lay pastors, lay pastor leaders, district pastors, and the senior pastor. No lay pastor can remain a lay pastor without submitting to this level of accountability through weekly reports.[8]

Rainer quotes Carl George who says, 'Have a change of mind about how ministry is to be done and a change of form in the infrastructure of the church.'

14.3 Structure around teams

When Nehemiah was rebuilding the walls of Jerusalem he organized the people to work in teams. We have a number of teams

---

[8] Rainer, *The Book of Church Growth*, p. 296.

that make up the ministry of our church. These, as with other small groups, are accountable to the church as a whole through other leadership teams appointed by the elders. Some of these teams are as follows:

- Pastoral Team
- Catering Teams (over 200 people)
- Sound System Team
- Reception Team for our 'drop-in' centre
- Cleaning Team
- Communion Preparation Team
- Youth Team
- Children's Workers Team
- Stewards Team
- Prayer Teams
- Finance Team
- Church Office Team
- Music and Worship Teams
- Ladies Ministry Team
- Parents and Toddlers Team
- Coffee Pot Team (our coffee shop)
- Bible Group Leaders Team (house groups)
- Missionaries' Support Teams
- Pastoral Assistants Team
- Banner Making Team
- Alpha Group Team
- Newcomers Team
- Towards Maturity Team
- Ministry Matters Team
- Information Table Team (Sundays)

These are not in any order of priority. They simply show how people are working, serving and exercising ministry together in ministry teams.

It is helpful to keep structures simple, as a barrier to growth in some UK churches is complexity. Even some small churches are so complex in their structures that they are their own worst enemy.

Members involved in the life and ministry of the local church need supporting, not only through encouragement and spiritual input, but also by providing practical support of material resources and tools. In a larger church this kind of support needs the daily availability of a church office.

14.4 Incorporate a church office

Office staff become increasingly necessary as the church grows. A church office can become the hub of daily or hourly communication and administration. If the church is serious about reaching the community, then the last thing to cut back is the infrastructure. The office needs to be available as a point of contact for both the community and the church. Leaders and ministry teams need to keep the office informed of what is happening and vice versa. The bigger the church grows the more likely it is that multiple office staff will be required for practical work such as answering the telephone; photocopying; producing letters, bulletins and other material for the church and ministry teams; gathering information; deciding what information is necessary, and when and where it is to be kept, produced or communicated. To avoid conflict and save time a flow of accurate information is vital in a growing church.

The office can become either a bottleneck or a facilitator of growth. Although it can be difficult for church members to understand its important role, the office should be thought of as being a ministry, and just like other ministry teams should express a servant heart towards both community and church.

Practise Your Purpose

15

Match Your Purpose to Your Potential

After applying the power, climbing to the designated altitude, keeping on course, coping with turbulence, and everything else that a pilot has to do, the reason for the flight should not be forgotten. The aircraft, having achieved its potential, has a purpose, which is to travel from one point to another and to arrive safely at the desired destination!

The church too must never forget its objective. How many times have meetings been held for the sake of the meeting itself? How often has a church become so preoccupied with all its departments and organization that it forgets why it exists? A church without a sense of purpose is a discouraged church, which soon becomes introspective and falls into another trap of trying to do too many things at once.

15.1 Remember no church can do everything

We feel guilty because we can't do everything we feel we should. There is always a pressure to do too many things. In one sense that's the way it should be. Christians with any kind of commitment will want to see God's work in the world flourish. Church members, therefore, will often have their own particular interests. In a church of 500 members all kinds of mission interests are present. A whole variety of mission organizations and agencies are represented and individually supported. Church members will often want their church to support their particular interest. I remember one small church that divided its surplus funds at the end of the financial year among 20 to 25 recipients, which meant that each mission or organization received about £10, because so many people wanted their interest represented. Would it not have been better to send all the £200 to one agreed agency, or even just two? This would have meant more substantial support from the church which could agree to support a different cause each year. At a church level that might be a more meaningful action.

The same problem arises at church meetings, when members feel strongly that their church should be involved in specific ministries that individual members have a heart for. The local church family is made up of people of all ages from many different backgrounds. Each age group will want their particular group in the community to be ministered to. We also remember that the church is about the only volunteer group that endeavours to look after, reach out to, and meet the needs of every age group, from cradle to grave. We live in a world of vast need. It's always been that way. Matthew's Gospel tells us that when Jesus

> saw the crowds, he had compassion on them, because they were harassed and helpless, like sheep without a shepherd. Then he said to his disciples, 'The harvest is plentiful but the workers are few. Ask the Lord of the harvest, therefore, to send out workers into his harvest field.' (Matthew 9:36–8)

We feel as Jesus did and we must obey his command to ask for more workers. In the meantime the danger is that we are diverted by many things from what God really wants us to focus on.

The church has a supreme purpose which is clearly defined in the Bible, but within that purpose it is necessary for each local church to fulfil its own particular purposes according to where God has planted it. We can't answer every call for help from the community, the nation and the world. We have to prioritize the particular purposes for our local church. This includes keeping a difficult balance between local community and world needs. The guilt can be intense for church leaders as members draw their attention to legitimate human needs. As appeals come from outside and inside the church to support a variety of ministries, the church has to decide just which ministries God has called it to assist.

We resolve the dilemma by defining our objectives. This is a process that motivates people and it's thrilling to see people become enthusiastic as they rediscover how God wants to use their church. Rick Warren says:

> Nothing discourages a church more than not knowing why it exists. On the other hand, the quickest way to reinvigorate a plateaued or declining church is to reclaim God's purpose for it to help members understand the great tasks the church has been given by Christ.[1]

It is important to take time over this process, otherwise you may have a set of purposes that is broad or unrealistic. Sometimes mission or purpose statements are too vague or too long for anyone to keep in mind. We can begin with a broad approach. For example, in an inspiring document *Five Core Values for a Gospel People* the Baptist Union of Great Britain recently called on its churches to be

A prophetic community
- Confronting evil, injustice and hypocrisy.
- Challenging human concepts of power, wealth, status and security.

---

[1] Rick Warren, *The Purpose-Driven Church*, Zondervan 1995, p. 87.

An inclusive community

• Transcending barriers of gender, language, race, class, age and culture.
• Identifying with those who are rejected, deprived and powerless.

A sacrificial community

• Accepting vulnerability, and the necessity of sacrifice.
• Seeking to reflect the generous, life-giving nature of God.

A missionary community

• Demonstrating in word and action God's forgiving and healing love.
• Calling and enabling people to experience the love of God for themselves.

A worshipping community

• Engaging in worship and prayer that inspires and undergirds all we are and do.
• Exploring and expressing what it means to live together as the people of God, obeying his word and following Christ in the whole of daily life.

Each of these core values contains suggested ways in which they may be expressed in the local church, in the denomination and in society. Under each of these objectives practical suggestions are given for the way each local church might apply the core values.

This still leaves churches to decide their priorities in their own specific circumstances. However, the overriding purpose of a church is to be a missionary congregation, reaching out to people of all ages with the 'ministry' and 'message' of 'reconciliation' (2 Corinthians 5:18–19).

The well-known Anglican church leader John Stott once described evangelism as:

part of God's mission through God's church in God's world. . . . It includes the kind of dialogue in which we listen humbly and sensitively in order to understand the other person. . . . It is the offer on the ground of the work of Christ, of a salvation which is present possession and future prospect. And it invites a total response of repentance and faith which is called conversion, the beginning of an altogether new life in Christ, in the church and in the world.

Evangelism professor Lewis Drummond defines evangelism as:

A concerted effort in the power of the Holy Spirit to confront unbelievers with the truth about Jesus Christ and the claims of our Lord (Acts 2:22–24, 31) with a view to leading unbelievers into repentance toward God and faith in our Lord Jesus Christ (Acts 20:21) and thus into the fellowship of His church so they may grow in the Spirit.[2]

Only when the church proclaims the gospel to its community in lifestyle and word can it be called the church.

15.2 Each church can do something

No church can do everything, but each church can do something significant. However, it is important to remember that to prioritize doesn't necessarily mean doing things in an order of priority. Just as our human bodies have several systems which must all run at the same time if we are to be healthy, so a church is healthy when the basic systems are all operating together. Just like a human body, when one system is not properly functioning, the rest of the body suffers. Worship, teaching, fellowship and evangelism are all systems to be up and running. So how do we prioritize?

---

[2] Lewis Drummond, *The Word of the Cross*, Broadman 1992, Introduction.

15.3 Twelve questions to help define your purpose

1. What are the things that we seem to do best as a church? What do we seem to be really good at?
2. What are the two biggest needs in our community?
3. Is there a predominant age group in our community that we should be reaching?
4. What is the age group we seem to be the most attractive to? Is this the age group we should be targeting, or should we be reaching a wider community?
5. Are we listening to the culture of our community?
6. What support groups could we set up in our community?
7. What kind of life experience is represented in our church that we could offer to the community?
8. What is the predominant culture of our community?
9. Are we reaching people for Christ and incorporating them into the church family?
10. What have been our most effective strategies for outreach?
11. Do we encourage and enable the spiritual growth and development of church members?
12. What are the predominant giftings in our church, which may indicate the ministries we should set up?

The answers received from these questions may indicate the kind of primary ministries the church should be offering and the kind of church culture that should be developed. The answers will help determine your priorities.

Try to express your purpose in one statement that can easily be remembered by the church membership. Make sure it is a statement that prompts you to ask if you are achieving it. Don't make it so broad or vague that it is easily forgotten and becomes meaningless. A good purpose statement not only defines what you will do, but also what you will not do.

A purpose statement is the beginning of your strategy. Ideally it needs to be followed with a mission statement which is a statement about *how* your purpose is to be achieved. The purpose statement is the 'what' and the mission statement is the 'how'. There is often confusion between a purpose statement and a mission statement. A purpose statement answers the question 'What are we here for?' A mission statement is about how the purpose will be achieved. Some churches confuse these two and as a consequence sometimes end up with a vague statement which is neither a mission nor a purpose statement. I would like to give examples, but fear I could embarrass the churches from which they come.

Next, what *programmes* do you need in order to achieve your mission? What will be the *goals* of these programmes? Then, what *strategies* do you need to reach the goals you have set? Write down, 'To achieve these goals we must . . .'

Finally, how will you *implement* the strategies? What training and recruiting do you need to do? A summary of that process would look like this:

- Purpose Statement
- Mission Statement
- Programmes
- Goals
- Strategies
- Implementation

Focus on fulfilling the purposes of the church. Keep watering and fertilising and cultivating and weeding and pruning. God will grow his church to the size he wants it, at the rate that's best for your situation.[3]

15.4 Churches together can do more

Churches associating and working together can achieve more in the community than churches working in isolation. I

---

[3] Warren, *The Purpose-Driven Church*, p. 394.

was once told that there are two things that bring churches together: danger or devotion. Certainly in the UK it is often the danger element that causes churches to work together: inner-city churches facing massive urban problems, a group of declining churches fighting for survival, or a whole nation of churches facing decline. In contrast, where churches choose to work together in areas where they are sufficiently strong on their own, much more can be achieved, providing they recognize each other's strengths and weaknesses, they do not see themselves in competition with each other, and they respect their differences.

There has been a particularly healthy co-operation between the churches in Frinton ever since 1891, when the town's population was only 75. Today, Frinton Area Churches Together consists of churches of varying denominations in which the churches and clergy work well together. Every year throughout the twentieth century they have worked together in a summer mission which has attracted children, youth and adults of all ages; visitors and residents.

Churches have made the greatest impact on a nation when they have crossed the denominational divides, eliminated competitiveness, and worked together in mission. Where local churches are able to co-operate with each other, each church can define and prioritize its purposes more clearly. Where one church lacks the gifts and experience, another church may be equipped with these. This enables a church to be honest enough to admit that there are needs it cannot address and aspects of mission it is not appropriate to support. Churches working together can meet a much greater range of community needs and together can make a much more effective impact. The unity of each local church can also be a model to the community. It is an even stronger role model when the unity and fellowship of several churches together is clearly visible.

In every church a sense of purpose is important. Members of

the congregation need to feel it each Sunday. Each worship service is not only a step in their own individual journey but also in the journey of the church. There are only 52 Sundays a year, but each is an opportunity to lead the church forward in its development. There is nothing so discouraging as routine worship services that seem to be going nowhere. When that happens people go to 'a service' and there is no sense of movement forward. Worship is simply perfunctory. This kind of atmosphere doesn't attract crowds.

Build a spiritual momentum that helps people understand in every worship service that the church is on a journey with God and with people. We are seeking to grow as individuals and a congregation in our relationship with God and with one another, and with the community and the world. This sense of expectation, journey and purpose is quickly detected by the visitor. In every church I have had the privilege of leading, this sense of journey, purpose and anticipation of the future has been a vital principle. I believe it is biblical. For example, Paul writes to the Colossians:

> We always thank God, the Father of our Lord Jesus Christ, when we pray for you, because we have heard of your faith in Christ Jesus and of the love you have for all the saints – the faith and love that spring from the hope that is stored up for you in heaven and that you have already heard about in the word of truth, the gospel that has come to you. All over the world this gospel is bearing fruit and growing, just as it has been doing among you since the day you heard it and understood God's grace in all its truth. (Colossians 1:3–6)

This sense of purpose must breathe through the whole church. Leith Anderson says:

> The external appearance of churches isn't everything, but it is a sign of health. Those superficial appearances of health include the upkeep of the church building, invitations to the unchurched by

church members, excitement in the hallways before and after services, and the sense that this church is alive and going somewhere. Just looking and listening goes a long way in concluding, 'This is a healthy church!'[4]

---

[4] Leith Anderson, *A Church for the Twenty-First Century*, Bethany House 1992, p. 142.

16

Reviewing the Priorities

On any flight, long or short, a pilot needs constantly to review the course heading, the power setting, the altitude, and the speed. For a pilot in radar and radio contact there is always outside help. In the dark, or in thick cloud, the constant monitoring of flight instruments is crucial, but many aircraft these days are equipped with a transponder. On it is a small light which shines brighter than the others. As one pilot put it, 'Every time that little light glows brighter, it means that somebody on the ground loves you.' An aircraft flight controller on the ground will give the pilot a special number that no other plane in the air at that time has. The pilot puts this number into the transponder. From then on, the people on the ground can identify that aircraft from all other aircraft. The light shines brighter every time the radar beam on the ground strikes the plane. It means that someone down there has the aircraft in view on a radar screen.

It may sound trite, but I believe every local church is on God's radar screen. He knows exactly where it is. The progress of the local church is at times difficult, demanding the combined efforts of people, leaders and the Holy Spirit. When the apostles came up against a difficult decision, after reviewing the priorities, they came to the point where they were able to say: 'It seemed good to the Holy Spirit and to us' (Acts 15:28). The Bible is full of occasions when this wonderful co-operation is seen.

God sees us, and it is a great comfort to know that while we are defining our particular purposes and reviewing our priorities, he is keeping track of us to guide us and keep us out of danger.

On the aircraft itself is an automatic pilot. The human pilot selects the direction in which he wants to fly, the altitude, and the power settings, then turns on the automatic pilot, takes his hands off the controls and the plane flies itself. The automatic pilot keeps the aircraft on course, at the correct altitude. But the human pilot can always override the automatic pilot and resume control of the aircraft when the situation demands it.

In many ways, surrendering the life of the church to the Holy Spirit's guidance is like putting an aircraft on autopilot. We do this by continually measuring our purposes and priorities against the Holy Spirit's direction, as best we know how. We continually pray that he will take over the direction of the church, fill it with his presence and energize it with his power.

We should rely totally on the Holy Spirit to give power and blessing to those principles which lead to building balanced, healthy, growing churches. A church filled with the person and power of the Holy Spirit is the most powerful force in the world today. One of the signs of a healthy church seeking to be a missionary congregation is that it will develop a willingness to review its structures and organizations regularly in order to assess its effectiveness in making known the good news of the gospel of Christ.

If we have set goals that are relevant, related to the needs of both the church and the community, we can be better aware of our strengths and weaknesses and the effectiveness of our ministries. As already noted, goals must be measurable. Vague goals which cannot be measured over a specified time frame are worthless. Good goal-setting will include a system of account-ability.

Our task is to build the church of Jesus Christ. How we do that in our particular culture and community will be unique to us, but it is certain that to be faithful to the New Testament we need continually to audit and monitor four areas:

1. Are we preaching the positive message of the gospel?
2. Are we equipping God's people for ministry?
3. Are we praying and planning for spiritual and numerical growth?
4. Are we implementing the purposes of our church?

The previous chapter summarizes a strategy for achieving the purposes of a church. Now add a further step in the strategy so that it looks like this:

- Purpose Statement
- Mission Statement
- Programmes
- Goals
- Strategies
- Implementation
- *Evaluation*

This last step means we reverse the strategy. Evaluation is a process built into the strategy of every healthy church. Ask the following questions: Are we *implementing* the strategies? Are the *strategies* enabling us to reach our goals? Are the *goals* fulfilling the programmes? Are the *programmes* achieving the *purposes* of the church?

Systems of appraisal are an important part of this process. All departments of church life need to be looked at and assessed. In a larger church it is sometimes necessary to appoint a small group of two or three people to appraise a particular ministry in the church. Leaders, of course, have a particular responsibility to review and evaluate.

Any review of church life must be done on biblical principles with objectivity, honesty, bravery and, above all, in the spirit of helpfulness, understanding and love. Much discussion and prayer needs to go into the process. The whole idea is for a local church to understand itself and all its activities in line with its purpose. Such a work must constantly go on but ultimately, it would be hoped, God's Spirit will so lead that his blessings will result in a far more effective ministry for the church with many more people won to Christ, discipled and equipped. The review must be more than a mere diagnostic exercise; the church must continually follow the Spirit in new methods of outreach and ministry to the glory of God. The rewards will be worth it!

May God motivate us to implement principles of church health and growth that will unleash the mighty potential of the church in the UK and across the world. My spiritual mentor Dr Lewis Drummond wrote: 'The world waits to hear the gospel communicated in power. If all the church can be mobilised, empowered, and equipped, it could be that this generation will really see "the evangelisation of the world".'[1]

---

[1] Lewis Drummond, *The Word of the Cross*, Broadman 1992, p. 333.

17

A Future for Your Church

There are many encouraging signs that the church in the UK is beginning to reach the unchurched. Alpha courses, and similar initiatives, are meeting not only on church premises and in homes, but in pubs, schools and factories. I know of at least one Alpha group that met in a McDonald's fastfood restaurant. The church is beginning to meet people on their own ground. In at least one town, the Salvation Army provided a Sunday school in a supermarket. More and more Christians are taking seriously their role in the workplace. In many churches there is a change of attitude towards being a church. Some Christians no longer see themselves as 'going to church' when they worship. Instead they are the church 'coming from the workplace', gathering together to worship. It is 'the church going to worship', rather than people 'going to church'.

There are encouraging signs that churches are becoming more sensitive to the unchurched visitor, trying to build bridges into the communities, and finding creative ways to help people make the journey from church-based weekday activities to sharing in worship.

There are encouraging signs too that Christians are witnessing to a holistic gospel; a growing willingness to share a biblical lifestyle; to meet the needs of the impoverished and vulnerable; and there is a greater emphasis on making disciples, not just building up numbers.

In all these things the church needs to be shaped by the four distinctives mentioned in Acts 2: 'They devoted themselves to the apostles' teaching and to the fellowship, to breaking of bread and to prayer' (Acts 2:42). As Rob Warner says in his book, Luke records four further distinctives of the Jerusalem church growing out of these four devotions:

- They enjoyed a lifestyle shaped by kindness and generosity.
- They enjoyed a vibrant worship.
- They enjoyed a lifestyle that was attractive to outsiders.
- They enjoyed sustained numerical growth through conversions.[1]

The church in Acts undoubtedly preached a positive message, equipped people for service and ministry, prayed for spiritual and numerical growth, and clearly understood their purpose.

In the twenty-first century there will be a greater variety of local churches. Some people believe that the local gathering of believers in a designated building will cease. In spite of declining attendances, there is no sign that local churches will disappear. On the contrary, throughout Western culture very large churches are coming into being. In the 1960s and 70s the demise of strong churches was frequently predicted, but at the end of the twentieth century there are growing numbers of very large churches. Most of them are not traditional, though some are, but with greater emphasis on worship and preaching being more visual and seeker-sensitive. More church leaders are committed to building larger churches. Terry Virgo, leader of the New Frontier churches in the UK, said in the 1980s, 'As we approach the 1990s we are praying and working toward

---

[1] Rob Warner, *21st-Century Church*, Kingsway 1999.

building larger churches that will reach out effectively into Great Britain, Europe, and the ends of the earth.' As mentioned in Chapter 7, the congregation of Kingsway International Christian Centre in Hackney, London, has grown from 300 to a staggering 5,000 in seven years! Victory Church in Finchley, and King's Church, Newport, are growing at extraordinary rates. Churches within established denominations including Holy Trinity, Brompton, and the Christian Centre, Sunderland, are experiencing and sustaining rapid growth. So-called 'warehouse' churches – congregations meeting in large former warehouses on industrial estates – are drawing larger numbers of people. These churches have the advantages of accessibility, car parking, purpose-designed buildings, high visibility, and flexibility. Then there are other more mainstream denominational churches such as our own that have grown to a regular Sunday congregation of 800 spread across three worship services.

Why do some churches grow while others decline? It could be argued that it is easier to grow churches in certain places, such as suburban or middle-class areas. But that's not the whole story. In many ways it is more difficult to grow a church in a town like Frinton which is relatively affluent and small. Jesus said, 'I tell you the truth, it is hard for a rich man to enter the kingdom of heaven. Again I tell you, it is easier for a camel to go through the eye of a needle than for a rich man to enter the kingdom of God' (Matthew 19:23–4). There are many attractions and distractions to keep affluent people from church. Some people find it harder to be a Christian in a small community where so many people know their lifestyle.

It is true, however, that larger churches are attractive to people who are comfortable with large social organizations. Leith Anderson says that larger churches

also have an appeal to people who seek anonymity, specialised services, or sophisticated programmes and methods. More megachurches are on the way since they fit well with a large part of the coming twenty-first-century culture and lifestyle.[2]

A new concept is the shopping-centre church. Though started in America it is coming to the UK as much as any other part of the world. It is built on the philosophy that the modern shopping centre has influenced the way the people think about how an institution ought to be. The shopping centre is 'the new town square, the community marketplace, the meeting place, the source of supplies, the place for entertainment, a major employer, and one of the few remaining common denominators in a fragmenting society.'[3] Every time I visit our local out-of-town supermarket and shopping centre I think what a lot we can learn as churches from these centres of activity. They are not only the new marketplace where John Wesley might have preached. They are powerful indicators of how our culture operates. Consequently some churches are considering the 'shopping centre' way of doing things. This kind of church will offer variety, convenience, anonymity and help if you need it. These are churches which say: 'You don't have to come to lots of meetings, but come to those activities that will help you meet your needs.'

'Shopping-centre churches intentionally provide more services than any one person needs. Those who go to these churches take friends with different needs, knowing that there will be a place for them.'[4]

The shopping-centre church places great emphasis on providing ministries that meet community needs. It thinks less about its own comfort and structures and more about whether it is connecting with where people are. They don't say, 'You can

---

[2] Leith Anderson, *A Church for the Twenty-First Century*, Bethany House 1992, pp. 54–5.

[3] *Ibid.*, p. 164.

[4] *Ibid.*, p. 170.

change your plan to fit our schedule,' but instead try to say, 'We'll change our schedule to fit your plans.'

Whatever we may think of the shopping-centre churches there is no doubt that changes are taking place in styles of worship, methods of outreach and mission, and church life generally in many independent churches and in nearly every mainstream denomination as well. Some of these changes are a struggle for us and are undoubtedly affected by modern Western culture.

The Win Arn Growth Report[5] included a list of contrasting styles, many of which apply as much to the UK as the USA, and you will find these 'old' and 'new' 'paradigms' reproduced on the next page. This list provides a picture of the perceived trends that will shape church culture in the twenty-first century.

There is a church in south London whose old building was burned to the ground several years ago. When they constructed the new building, they discovered that they could use the old foundations. They now have a newer building, built and equipped for today's ministry, but it is built on the old foundations. It is a reminder to us that we need not be afraid of change; indeed we should welcome those changes prompted by the Holy Spirit to meet today's needs, as long we build

on the foundation of the apostles and prophets, with Christ Jesus himself as the chief cornerstone. In him the whole building is joined together and rises to become a holy temple in the Lord. And in him you too are being built together to become a dwelling in which God lives by his Spirit. (Ephesians 2:20–22)

[5] *Ibid.*, pp. 150–151

OLD	NEW
Effective Evangelism	
Confrontational	Relational
Mass	Personal
General population	Specific 'people groups'
Single presentation	Multiple exposure
Single method	Multiple methods
Goal: a decision	Goal: a disciple
America: a Christian nation	America: a secular field
Church membership	Church discipleship
Motive: guilt	Motive: value and love
Pastor and Staff	
Enabler	Initiator
Activity-oriented	Achievement-oriented
Teaching style: propositional	Teaching: experiential
Selection based on credentials and denominational history	Selection based on performance
Church staff drawn from seminary	Church staff drawn from congregation
Christian Education	
Sunday school	Small groups
Age-graded	Lifestyle-graded
One weekly meeting time and place	Numerous meeting times and places
Verbal-oriented	Visual-oriented
Paid youth director	Staff with youth and other tasks
Senior Adults	
Requires volunteers	Source of volunteers
Care-takers	Care-givers
Apathetic outreach to seniors	Intentional outreach to seniors
One senior adult group and programme	Multiple senior adult groups and programmes
Retirement motive: play	Retirement motive: work, learn, serve and play
Facilities	
Considered adequate	Regularly upgraded

OLD	NEW
Worship	
Presentation	Participation
Intellectual	Experiential
Focus on Christians	Focus also on non-Christians
Volunteers	
Sacrifice self	Maximize self
Members serve institution	Institution serves members
Volunteers	Paid employees
The Denominational 'System'	
Resists change	Insists on change
Centralized	Regionalized
Bureaucracy	Accountability
Served by churches	Serves churches

We should be concerned about numbers, as they represent people. Derek Tidball, Principal of the London Bible College, wrote in the *Baptist Times*:

> The growth of the church is about much more than numbers. But the New Testament repeatedly refers to a growth in numbers as a sign of the progress of the gospel. So, what are we so apologetic about? Too often we are told we are called to faithfulness not success. But we are called to be stewards, and stewards are not being faithful if they let their Master's assets decline. If Christ is truly Lord and the Holy Spirit is genuinely at work we shall have a passion to make disciples and see people converted.

There is a distinction between 'church growth' which is natural to the New Testament, and the 'church growth movement' about which some people are sceptical. Yet the church growth movement has obviously had a positive impact on many church leaders. To me it is significant that church growth, as a modern-day movement, began with the work of a missionary, Donald McGavran. Born in India in 1897, and inspired by such pioneers as William Carey, McGavran spent much of his ministry studying what makes churches grow. He went to America for his college and postgraduate education and in 1923 returned to India as a missionary appointed by the United Christian Missionary Society. He researched the lack of growth among Indian churches and published his results in 1936; but did further research until 1955, when he wrote *The Bridges of God*, the result of 20 years of investigating church growth. Little did he realize that his book would mark the beginning of a new major missiological movement. Donald McGavran reiterated time and time again that God wanted his lost sheep found and brought into the field. His biblical mandate was the Great Commission to 'go and make disciples of all nations'.

But we must not forget the great spiritual awakenings of the seventeenth and eighteenth centuries. Such leaders as John Wesley, George Whitefield, William Carey, Charles Spurgeon, William Booth, Hudson Taylor and D. L. Moody are part of our evangelical heritage. These leaders, together with major movements of the Holy Spirit throughout the modern world, are still significant influences on church growth in the twenty-first century.

I believe there is a future for thousands of churches all over the UK if they implement biblical principles of being the church. In the final analysis, church health and growth has to do with attitude. William Carey, the father of modern missions, made the famous statement which still inspires and challenges us: 'Expect great things from God. Attempt great things for God.'

Recommended Reading

Anderson, Leith, *A Church for the Twenty-first Century – Bringing Change to Your Church to Meet the Challenges of a Changing Society,* Bethany House Publishers, Minneapolis, 1992.

Chalke, Steve and Radford, Sue, *New Era, New Church?* Harper Collins, London, 1999.

Cymbala, Jim, *Fresh Wind, Fresh Fire*, Zondervan, Michigan, 1997.

Drummond, Lewis A., *The Word of the Cross – Contemporary Theology of Evangelism*, Broadman Press, Nashville, 1992.

George, Carl F., *How to Break Growth Barriers – Capturing Overlooked Opportunities for Church Growth*, Baker Book House, Grand Rapids, 1993.

Hill, Mike, *Reaching the Unchurched*, Scripture Press, Harpenden, 1994.

Hybels, Lynne and Bill, *Rediscovering Church – the Story and Vision of Willow Creek Community Church*, Zondervan, Michigan, 1995.

Rainer, Thom S., *The Book of Church Growth*, Broadman & Holman, Nashville, 1993.

Richter, Philip and Francis, Leslie J., *Gone but not Forgotten – Church Leaving and Returning*, Darton, Longman & Todd, London, 1998.

Schwarz, Christian A., *Natural Church Development – A Guide to Eight Essential Qualities of Healthy Churches*, Church Smart Resources, 1996, available in the UK through the British Church Growth Association.

Wagner, C. Peter, *Leading Your Church to Growth*, Regal, Ventura, 1984.

Warner, Rob, *21st-Century Church*, Kingsway, Eastbourne, 1999.

Warren, Rick, *The Purpose-Driven Church – Growth Without Compromising Your Message or Mission,* Zondervan, Michigan, 1995.